TIME 4

HIGH SCHOOL©
Time Management
Student Workbook

Elizabeth Franklin

TIME 4 HIGH SCHOOL©
Time Management
Student Workbook
(Revision of TIME 4 KIDS and TEENS© 2009)

Illustrations by Morgan Pope
Cover Illustration provided by www.FreeDigitalPhotos.net
Public Domain Clip Art from pdclipart.org
Some quotes on time from www.specialty-calendars.com

Copyright © 2009 by:
Elizabeth Franklin
P.O. Box 194
Strawberry Plains, TN 37871
www.time2BGREAT.com

Published in the United States of America
ISBN 145057033X
EAN-13 is 9781450570336.

This book is dedicated to...
all the greatness hidden inside this young
generation.

May you find TIME to do the GREAT
things!

Table of Contents

A Note to Teachers...

TIME 4 HIGH SCHOOL© is designed to introduce pre-college and college age students to good time management skills and encourage prioritizing time choices. It also is designed to inspire and encourage a healthy self-image as well as more family time interaction.

TIME 4 HIGH SCHOOL© is suitable for the life challenges facing high school students as well as for pre-college planning. I would recommend copying charts so they can be used throughout the year to monitor improvement. These could be used year after year as tools to help manage time, especially in school.

Habits take time to form. Home life can greatly affect success or failure in this course. I suggest requiring a daily TO DO List and Weekly Planning from each student. Approach this in a manner to not be cumbersome, but to fit each personality type. Though they will want to try each form, let them choose which kind to maintain every day. One student may be laid back and doing a simple jotted down list is an accomplishment. To a type A personality student, he or she may thrive with detailing a daily plan. The TO DO List that is both written out and *used* everyday is the one that works!

I also suggest establishing a reward program for this course to acknowledge life style changes. If you see a student making notes of homework assignments, looking at his calendar to see what is planned, and taking responsibility for time in new ways; encourage their lifestyle changes with age appropriate rewards.

You will find a list of student success hot points in the back of the workbook. I use it for an outline for "Time Talks" with young people. It would be good to read through these at the beginning of the course with students to get some basic pointers and see where they are going in the course.

There is a chapter on college preparation in the back chapters. Hopefully, by that point students will already have time skills in place and can begin to look forward into the challenges of college life. You will also find an answer key for chapter quizzes in the back of the workbook.

Thanks for taking the TIME to teach this young generation the value of TIME.

TIME

empower you to be great by teaching you how to manage your time.

I believe wholeheartedly in your generation. I have faith it will be the greatest generation this world has ever known! With our fast paced society and high technology, you will be required to learn good time management skills. The level of freedom that avails teenagers and college students today demands more control of your minutes. The level of responsibility required in college demands more control of your minutes.

The good news is— you can get it all done and still have fun in college. This course will give you basic lessons in time management, will challenge your perspective of life, and encourage you to greatness in your lifetime. Let's begin our journey into success!

If you're approximately 20 years old, you have somewhere around 50 years left here on earth. That's 18,212 days. What you do with the rest of your life will be determined <u>one</u> day at a time.

In these next pages we will probe your priorities, your time fillers and wasters, your desires, and hopefully, you will finish this course with a sense of hope and new awareness for your time.

QUOTE OF THE DAY
"By failing to prepare you are preparing to fail."
Benjamin Franklin

BE A TIME SLEUTH

For the first few days of this course, take a little time to find out the pros and cons of planning. Be a "time sleuth" and find out just who needs time management.

Talk to a business owner, teacher, coach, your doctor or dentist, and your parents. How do they get everything done? Do they see value in planning? Do they plan and keep TO DO lists? Does planning make a difference in their lives?

Experiment with a day totally unplanned, a day planned out in your mind, and a day with a plan written down. Which day was most successful?

After this week, each Monday you will need to do a written plan for each week. Also, everyday you will need to complete a TO DO List.

Why take the time to do all this planning? It has been proven that you are 30% more likely to do a task if it is written down. It will also make your day smoother. Plus, you will be developing life skills that will help you succeed at anything in life!

YOUR INTERNAL TIME CLOCK

Let's find out if your internal clock is accurate. Ask someone to time you for this test. Close your eyes and when you think one minute has passed, raise your hand. Using a stopwatch, have your helper see how close to an actual minute you raise your hand.

Did you raise your hand before the full minute?
Most likely, you THINK you can do more than you can because your estimation of time is too short. This would cause you to take on more than you can accomplish and feel overloaded because you try to squeeze 60 seconds into 45.

Did you raise your hand after the minute passed?
This could cause you be slow to respond. If your parents say you are leaving in five minutes, you may still be playing video games because you didn't realize five minutes had passed.

You can RESET your internal clock. Use a timer with a buzzer. Begin the timer and try to estimate the correct passage of one minute. Without watching the countdown to 0, try to raise your hand just as the buzzer sounds. After doing this experiment a few times, you will begin to accurately determine one minute and reset your internal clock!

II.
TO DO
LISTS

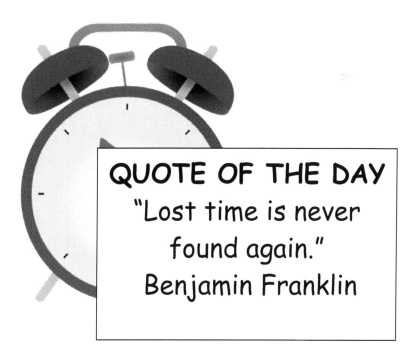

QUOTE OF THE DAY
"Lost time is never found again."
Benjamin Franklin

EXPERIMENT

SACCADIC EYE MOTION

Ask a test subject to draw a large imaginary circle with their eyes, without moving their head. Watch the motion of their eyes. Is it a smooth circle? No, you will find the motion to be choppy and jagged.

Now, stand in front of the person and draw a big circle in the air with your finger. Ask your test subject to follow your finger. Watch the eyes of your test subject. Do they go in a smooth circle? Yes! Why???

This is called saccadic eye motion. Your eyes need a pattern to follow to accomplish what they want to do. Your brain is the same way. It needs a pattern to follow to do what it wants to do today! That's why you need "TO DO" lists and weekly plans. It gives your brain a pattern to follow.

II. TO DO LISTS

We will discuss weekly planning later but let's start at the beginning. The first step in time management is learning about TO DO Lists. You can simply jot down a list, use a form like the one on page 12 or design your own. If you would like a colorful one to customize each day, go to www.workingmom.com. You can make a customized TO DO List to print out after filling in your information. For today, do a simple handwritten list for a TO DO List. You can choose what works best for you.

What is a TO DO List? It is a list of everything you intend or need to accomplish today. Your TO DO List is a commitment— to *yourself*. If you can't keep your commitments to yourself, how do you expect to keep them toward others? TO DO Lists help teach personal responsibility.

Start out easy! Take 2 minutes to quickly jot down all the things you need "to do" today. Use a highlighter to mark the items listed that <u>must</u> be done before the day is through. As you complete each task, draw a line through it. TA-DA! You just did a TO DO List!

COLOR CODE YOUR JOBS

Ask your parents to buy an inexpensive calendar that is big enough for you to write in the squares, or print one off on the computer.

Assign soccer, dance, club meetings, school, etc. its own color that will be used with everything about that subject. Using a colored marker, list all of your dance practices in pink with a matching pink dance bag. Mark soccer practices and games in your team color, perhaps blue, on your calendar. Use a marker that matches your blue jersey. Also, buy a soccer bag in the same color to store your shin guards, balls, uniforms, and shoes. When you look at the calendar, you quickly identify "dance" by pink or "soccer" by blue and all the related events.

For school, make colored folders for each subject and use the folder for homework, research info, tests, etc. If science is green, use a green folder for all your work. When you write an assignment on your calendar, do it in green. When you see green on the calendar, it will always mean science related.

Color-coding is an easy way to make keeping up with your life, school, and extra curricular activities easier. It may seem a bit elementary, but even adults use color coding to facilitate order.

A NEW HABIT

Every day in this course, the first thing you will do is make a TO DO List for your day. At first it might be hard. It might seem it would be easier just to get to work and forget the TO DO List but it will pay off if you will stick with it!

Remember these things:
- You are 30% more likely to do something simply by writing it down.
- It will give your day more control.
- You won't get off track or forget assignments or appointments so easily.
- You will feel less stressed having a plan for your day.
- You will feel like you have accomplished something when you check off each item.

Now that you've learned the simple steps - DO THEM! Do important things first. If your list is impossible – ask for your parent or teacher's help to eliminate or reschedule something.

Are you willing to commit to this change for the 21 days required to make it a habit?

_____ yes   _____ no

SIMPLIFY YOUR TO DO LIST

Write down only the things you must do and can realistically accomplish today.

Make a SEPARATE LIST for things you need to do next week or later that week.

Categorize- A for absolutely need to get done things, B for lesser important, and C for least

Attack your list with wisdom- If you need to go to the library for a research paper, return books at the same time.

Get a distraction free time for concentration for homework. We will discuss this more later. Quiet, non-distracting study environments increase long term memory ability.

Finish a task before moving on. It is easier to finish homework in one sitting rather than spreading it out with breaks in between. Each time you stop requires time to get refocused.

Plan ahead of time. It is a best TO PLAN THE NIGHT BEFORE to separate the planning from the implementation of the plan.

QUIZ 1
To Do Lists

1. Why do we need to plan?

2. You are (A) 20%, (B) 30%, (C) 70% more likely to accomplish a task just by writing it down.

3. A TO DO List is a commitment to _____.

4. You should write your TO DO List on
(A)   separate pieces of paper for each job,
(B)   a list on one piece of paper.

5. Why should you sort a TO DO List into A, B, Cs?

6. How long does to take to form a new habit?

7. When is the best time to plan your day?
   A. The night before
   B. First thing in the morning
   C. At lunch
   D. As you do it

STUFF TO DO!!!

NAME_____	S	M	T	W	R	F	S
_____							
_____							
_____							
_____							
_____							

NAME_____	S	M	T	W	R	F	S
_____							
_____							
_____							
_____							
_____							

NAME_____	S	M	T	W	R	F	S
_____							
_____							
_____							
_____							

NAME_____	S	M	T	W	R	F	S
_____							
_____							
_____							
_____							
_____							

NAME_____	S	M	T	W	R	F	S
_____							
_____							
_____							
_____							
_____							

FUN FACT

The average
person spends:
5 years
waiting in line

6 years eating

2 years playing
telephone tag

1 year looking for
misplaced objects

6 months waiting
at red lights
in his lifetime.

III. PLANNING

QUOTE OF THE DAY
"Plans must be
simple and flexible....
They must be made
by the people
who execute them."
George S. Patton, Jr.

III. PLANNING

Now that you have a TO DO List, when do you do what? If you PLAN to do first things first, you will not only succeed in school but should also have time for the extracurricular and social times.

Planning means several things. Planning involves TO DO Lists and GOALS. A GOAL is something you intend to do, usually more long range than a TO DO List.

Planning involves expectations of teachers, parents, coaches, and of yourself. It also involves learning who you are and when you function best. First things first— Let's PLAN around you!

Plan your day as closely to your natural body clock as possible for maximum potential. PLAN to work on things that need high *concentration* during your peak times if possible and things that do not need so much concentration in your weaker times. If you have options on class times, consider scheduling harder subjects during your most productive, alert times. Try to work on homework during higher concentration times. You will accomplish more during your peak performance times and finish it more quickly.

STARTING TO PLAN

One thing to realize about time planning is that you are not the only person that has to be considered. Your time will be directly related to other people in your family. Planning is a communication tool to help make the family work better together.

Sunday night might be a good time to do weekly family planning. Put your time commitments for the week on the family calendar.

Ask yourself questions like:

1. What time commitments do I have this week?

2. What time commitments do other siblings or my parents have that involves my time?

3. Where do I have to be and when?

4. Do I have any special school projects this week that will need extra time?

5. Do I have any plans with friends this week?

6. Do I have any extra sports/church/dance practices or meetings this week?

DO I NEED A PLANNER?

What exactly is a "Daily Planner"? It is a place to record important appointments that you don't want to miss. In business, a person will record all his appointments with clients, meetings, deadlines, and important family events.

Suppose you told your dad last week that you were playing in the basketball finals for your team next Thursday afternoon. It's an important game to you and you want your dad to be there.

Just suppose, your dad tries to keep up with everything he needs to do remember in his head. He makes a mental note of it and goes off to work. The following Monday, after a busy weekend, your dad is in an appointment with a client. They agree to meet and close the deal later in the week. The client looks at his calendar and says he can meet Thursday after noon or late Friday evening. You dad has an option as to when to set the appointment.

Since he didn't write down the basketball game and it has been an entire week since you talked about it, he forgets the time of the game. He schedules this big business appointment on Thursday afternoon. How would that make you feel?

What would help your dad in that situation? A Daily Planner would help him keep up with all his time commitments.

As you get in college and working, you will have more and more time obligations to remember. You can keep a daily planner or use the calendar on your ipod. Suppose a friend invites you to go out. If you have carefully recorded all your time obligations, you can pull out your planner and check to see what day is free for you and not overlap other important things on your schedule.

Perhaps you take several days of dance in classes that start at varying times. A planner keeps you at the right class and the right time. Look at your planner in the morning as you make your TO DO List. If you record all your rehearsals, sports practices, as soon as you are given the schedule, it is done for the entire season.

If you choose a small planner, it will fit in your purse or back pocket. At school you can use it for homework assignments and things you have to remember for classes. Usually there is enough room to do a TO DO List on the day as well, bringing all your time tools into one place. Buy a simple planner to use in this course.

FAMILY PLANNER

Do you get tired of your little brother or sister interfering with your plans? You invite friends over for an Xbox night only to walk in and find your kid sister has a bunch of little girls in for a sleepover. How do you avoid that? Ask your parents to do a family schedule for the week.

Using calendar page, have each person in your family write down all extra-curricular activities: soccer practice, library, dance, church, sleep-overs, special projects due, meetings, etc. for the week.

Discuss which trips might require you to provide transportation for a younger sibling and which events you will be required to attend. See how the schedule is going to affect all the other family members.

PLAN YOUR TIME!

If you plan to do first things first, you will have time for the extracurricular and social times. In college you will receive a syllabus that shows all your requirements for every class for the entire semester. If your teacher has a syllabus for your class assignments this week, ask for a copy. Record all the assignments, test, and homework into your planner. If you don't use a syllabus, experiment with this type of planning using a research project or science fair project.

Where is Your Time Going?

To most of us time is like sand slipping through our fingers. It's time to catch that sand! We're going to look for some TIME THIEVES. How many hours daily/weekly do you spend in each area below:

_____ (35) Class
_____ (10) School- Homework, Research, Meetings
_____ (56) to (70) Sleep (8-10 hrs pr night x7)
_____ (14) Eating (2 hrs daily x7)
_____ (7) Personal (1 hr daily- shower/hair, etc)
_____ (7) Household Chores (1 hour daily)
_____ (6) Athletics/Youth Group/Scouts/Events

Add these up to see how many hours weekly do you spend on these "essentials"? _____

What's Left?

There are 168 hours in a week. How many hours per week do you have left over to choose what you do with your time?

168- ____(essentials) = choice time_____

Think about your day yesterday. What did you plan to do? What did you really do?

	What I wanted to do	**What I did do**
6-9 AM		
10-12 AM		
1-3 PM		
4-6 PM		
7-9 PM		
9-12 PM		

REALITY CHECK:
If you go to school full time
and are on a sports team,
you will be at school more hours each week
than an adult who works a full time job!
You need to manage your TIME!

IV. GOALS

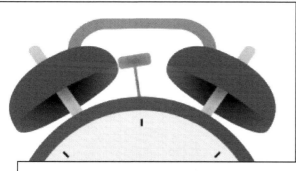

QUOTE OF THE DAY
"Dost thou love life,
Then do not squander time,
For that's the stuff
Life is made of."
Benjamin Franklin

IV. LET'S MAKE SOME GOALS!

Have you ever wished you had a new game system, could make a new friend, make straight A's at school, or dreamed of doing beautiful pirouettes or scoring goals like a famous soccer star? That dream or wish can stay a "I wish I could" thing all of your life and never happen. How do you get what you wish for?

Goals are the process of moving a dream or a wish to a reality. When it is something you really, really want; you are willing to do the work to turn that dream or wish into a reality. The first step is to make it a goal.

Goals are like the motor behind your wishes and dreams. Setting a goal is like putting a battery in a remote control car. The car is designed to move, but it just sits there until you put in the battery. It is the same way with a special wish or a dream in your heart. It will just sit there as long as it stays only a wish.

You have to take your wish or dream, make it a goal, do the steps to get there, work hard, and persevere (keep on keeping on) until one day you see it come to pass. If you will stick with it, someday you will find yourself doing what you dreamed in your heart and were designed to do just like that remote control car was designed to move.

Goals motivate us to ACT. A goal helps us establish deadlines and define what we wish and dream about. By setting goals, we have an increased motivation (desire to do it) and incentive (reason to do it). Goals help us to focus our lives and keep on track.

Turning a wish or dream into a reality usually doesn't happen overnight. So how do we get from a wish to a reality? Let's look at the steps from a wish to a reality for a few different things:

1. Write it down- remember you are 30% more likely to accomplish something simply by writing it down. What are the things you wish or dream about in your heart? You may think your dream or wish is impossible and you could never get there. Take a few minutes to write down your dreams and wishes right now. Sometimes your heart dreams and goals are very personal. No one else has to look at your list if you want to keep it private.

My dreams and wishes:

I wish I could _____

_____

_____

_____

_____

Let's make a pretend list to walk you through the goal setting process:

I wish I ….

- Would win the new ipod they are giving away at the summer reading program at the library
- Had a horse
- Could dance in The Nutcracker performance
- Could help the hungry children in the world

2. The next step is taking that wish and making it a goal. A goal is something I want badly enough that I am willing to work at it.

My goals are:
To win that ipod in the reading program
To get my own horse
To dance in the Nutcracker
Help feed hungry children

3. Now you have to count the cost before you get started. This might take some research. For the summer reading program, do you remember how many books the winner read last year? Could you ask the librarian? For the horse, how much does it cost? What are the requirements to dance in the Nutcracker? Do you need to be at a certain skill level or studio? To feed hungry children, what programs are available that do this

that I might be able to help? How much does it cost?

Count the Cost for my goals:
- I need to read more than 305 books to beat last year's winner.
- I need $300-500 to buy my horse and lessons to know how to care for it and ride
- The person in charge of the Nutcracker is Mrs. Jones. I have to move to a different studio to be part of the Nutcracker. I have to be able to do a perfect pirouette to try out.
- Feed a Child costs $25 per month.

4. Now that I have my dreams and wishes written down into goals and considered the cost for my goals, I have to make a decision. **Do I want it badly enough to do what is needed to get there?** At this point, don't look at what you *don't have*. Once there was a woman who was losing her house because she could not pay the mortgage. She asked a wise man to help her. He said, "What do you have in your house?" She didn't have money for the mortgage, but she could make a special oil that others needed. He told her to sell the oil and she had enough to pay the mortgage. What do you have in your hands right now that might make your goal a reality? Perhaps you have a guitar you never play, or a four-wheeler you

have out grown that you could sell to buy your horse? You will never get to your goals if you focus on the things you don't have. Simply establish the goal and look for possibilities.

5. Believe in yourself and that you really can get to your goal. Your words are the rudder of your life ship. Do you know what a rudder does? It tells the ship where to go. You words are the same way for your goal. What are you saying about it? If you are always saying, " I really would like to have a horse but I know I'll never get one. Or I'll never have enough money for it," you are probably right. However, if you train your mouth to say the right things, it will set your mind into exploring the ways to make it happen. You could change that statement to, "I would really like to have a horse and I am certain that one day I will. I don't have enough money YET but I am going to get the money for my horse somehow." Do you see how that would change the way you see the possibility of it happening?

When my older son was about six he asked for a hamster. I told him he was too young for a hamster. It required a lot of care and he would have to do it himself when he got one. On the way to school one morning, I told him, "You can do anything you believe you can do." That afternoon he got in the car after school and said, "Let's go get my hamster." I looked at him with a confused look. "Mom, you said I can do anything I think I can do and I think I can take care of a hamster." Needless to say, he did get the hamster. He did take care of it, too.

6. Now, you have moved your wish or dream into a goal, considered the cost and decided to pay the price, written it down, and begun to say positive things about it. **The next step is to make the goal not seem so big and impossible.** To do this, break the goal into small steps you can reach one by one to get to the big goal. Think through what the steps may be to get to each of your dreams.

In our examples the steps might look something like this:
I am going to get my own horse. I need to save $300-$500 and learn to care for it.

Steps to take:
- Ask my parents if I can take riding/horse care lessons or get that for my birthday present
- Get the things I need for a horse
Halter-$20
Lead rope-$25
Brushes and Hoof Pick- $40
Saddle- Used $150 New $300

(You might buy a small thing for your horse to hang in your room to remind you every day that you are getting a horse.)

- Check to see what video games I don't play much that I could sell for my horse fund
- SAVE my allowance instead of buying things each week.
- Tell my grandparents or aunts and uncles that I really want a horse and would enjoy something for my horse or a contribution to my horse fund as an alternative to buying a gift.
- Could I earn money around the house doing extra jobs for my parents or get a part time job?
- Do I have any creative gifts that I could use to make things to sell for my horse fund?

In the Nutcracker dance example:
Steps to take:
- Talk to my parents about changing studios
- Check to see if the prices for lessons are the same at the other studio.
- Go check it out and see if I like the teachers and studio
- Begin to practice pirouettes 30 minutes every day

In the summer reading program example:

- I have 6 weeks in the summer reading program and need to read at least 305 books.
- Read 51 books each week-or about 7 or 8 per day.
- Set times to go to the library 3 time a week to check out books- I can only get 20 each time
- It takes me about 10 minutes per book, so I need to set aside 1 hour and 15 minutes each day to read
- 11-12:15 is going to be my reading time every day
- I will read my books before turning on the TV or videos each day

Do you see how 7 books a day seems less overwhelming than 305 books for the summer? If you reach your little daily goal, you will get to the big goal at the end of the summer.

Finally, in the feeding hungry children example:

I want to help feed hungry children
Steps to take:

- Find out on the web what programs feed hungry children (get parents permission first!)
- It is $25 per month to feed a child
- I will put $\frac{1}{2}$ of my allowance toward this and see if I can do odd jobs to earn money at home
- I will hold a car wash each month to make money for the children

- Make a feed the children box and go to my neighbors and see if they will give me some change to help the children

- Set up a checking account so I can deposit it in the bank and write a check to the organization

7. Next, you need to **set a deadline** (the time to finish something.) In the library example, the timing is easy. There is a specific time to turn in your list for the contest. Be sure to write that date on your calendar so you won't forget to get your list to the library on time!

For the horse, determine when you want to get your horse. If you know you can save $10 per week, divide the average cost by your weekly savings. That would mean in 30 weeks you would have $300 for a horse.

For dancing in the Nutcracker, you will need to find out how soon you need to switch studios to be considered for the performance. Find out when tryouts may be scheduled. You must perfect your pirouette before that date.

For feeding hungry children, establish a time to start sending money. Schedule all your fundraising events to be able to send in money by your deadline.

8. Finally, get to work! You have moved your wish or dream into a goal, considered the cost and decided to pay the price, written it down, are believing and saying positive things about it, and broken it down into small steps to accomplish little things to get to the big thing, what next? WORK at it, STICK with it, KEEP ON keeping on until it become a reality. Nothing worth having is cheap. It takes time and commitment. Greatness isn't cheap, but it's worth the investment of your TIME.

LITTLE KIDS CAN DREAM BIG

My youngest daughter, Anna, was five years old when she saw an ad about the children in Africa on TV. She wanted to help. She took all her savings from her piggy bank and asked me to send it to the children.

I knew a missionary, so I asked her how to help the children. She gave me a list of orphanages in India, Africa, and Central America who had no outside help financially. I contacted one in India, and found out he only needed $50 per month to feed all his orphans rice twice daily.

Anna began to save money. She asked the church to put a jar for change on a table in the foyer. She set up a change jar at her dad's work. Finally, she asked the neighbors if they would save their change for the hungry children. She collected change each weekend from the neighbors who agreed to help.

Anna fed the entire orphanage from her change collecting for two years until a church began to sponsor the orphanage and did not need the help. We also helped fix their house when floods damaged it, bought blankets to send, and sent Christmas gifts.

FROM WISH TO REALITY

I had always donated my daughter's outgrown clothing to Good Will. She was very gentle on her clothes so they always looked like new. When I was unpacking from a move, I noticed a bag of her shoes I had failed to take to Good Will.

That day, a missionary from Africa sent a Christmas newsletter. She mentioned going to pick up the children in her jeep because it was so far to walk and the children had no shoes. I thought, "I wish I could get the shoes in Anna's closet over to them."

It was a wish that would not go away. It just burned in my heart. I decided to start collecting really nice used clothes from moms when their children outgrew them to send to children like the ones in Africa who didn't have anything. I emailed the missionary from Africa to ask about how to do something like that.

She thought it was a wonderful idea. She had a ministry there in Africa that distributed clothes to the needy children. It had started when her daughter had been killed in a car accident. She had given away all her daughter's clothes to the needy after her daughter's death. Do you know the name of the ministry? ANNA'S CLOSET! The shoes that had started that wish in my heart were in my daughter, ANNA'S closet.

Since then I've gathered and sent clothing all over the world. We even took vanloads of children's clothing to Biloxi, Mississippi when Hurricane Katrina destroyed the area. Anna collected small stuffed animals to take. She cut out hearts on paper and wrote "I CARE" on the heart and tied them around the necks of the little bears. She handed them out to children that had lost all their toys and clothes in the hurricane.

When you have a dream or wish in your heart, don't let it die! Set it as a goal and work at it until it becomes a reality! You can do great things like this, too!

A good place to start learning the process of setting goals and breaking them into steps, setting deadlines, and working to see them done is in your schoolwork. A research paper or other large assignment is a GOAL to accomplish. Use the following page as a guide to breaking down a large assignment and get it done! Make copies of this page and use it for BIG projects and assignments to help you follow through!

Use this same process with your other goals in life!

GREATNESS is
Hiding inside
Each and
Every one
Of YOU!

Dream BIG dreams!

GOAL/ASSIGNMENT

_____

Estimated time for completion:_____
(Time Clue: ASK your teacher average time needed)

Due Date:_____

	How Long will this step take?	Target Date to finish this step
Step 1		
Step 2		
Step 3		
Step 4		
Step 5		

Project Date completed_____

DREAM⇒
GOAL⇒
REALITY

Let's Review the
 Goal Setting Steps:

1. Take a dream or wish
2. Set a goal
3. Count the cost
4. Believe in it
5. Say the right things
6. Find the small steps
7. Do them one by one
8. Work hard
9. Stick with it
10. See it become a reality!

QUIZ 2
PLANNING

1. Why should you talk to others in your family when making plans?

2. Planning involves _____ lists and weekly _____.

3. When should you study your more difficult subjects?

4. How does your natural body clock affect learning?

5. What is a "GOAL"?

> "I never did anything
> worth doing
> by accident
> nor did any
> of my inventions
> come by accident."
> Thomas Edison

V.
PRIORITIES

QUOTE OF THE DAY Cling
to the flying hours; and yet
Let one pure hope,
one great desire,
Like song on dying lips, be set,
That ere we fall
in scattered fire,
Our hearts may lift the
world's heart higher.
Edmund W. Gosse

V. PRIORITIES

This module is designed to help you realize what is important about time to you.   Life is choices. Everyday we are confronted by decisions to how to spend our time.

What are your Priorities?

Each decision is an irreversible choice. We cannot go back and recapture time that is lost. Beside the following areas, number them according to their importance to you, with #1 being the most important and #6 being the least.

___SCHOOL___WORK ___FAMILY ___GOD
___SPORTS/MUSIC ___FRIENDS

Showing what you value is what you *do* more than what you say. Using the same categories, write down the approximate number of hours per day you spend exclusively in the above areas, first on weekdays, then on weekends:

Weekdays:
___SCHOOL___WORK____FAMILY____GOD___
_SPORTS/MUSIC___FRIENDS ____FITNESS

Weekends:
___SCHOOL___WORK____FAMILY____GOD___
_SPORTS/MUSIC___FRIENDS____FITNESS

What surprises you about how you spend your time compared to how you rate your priorities of life? What would you do differently?

What Is Your "Keeper"?

You have just been told that everything in your life *EXCEPT FOR ONE THING* will be gone forever. What would be the one thing you would maintain above everything else in your life? Would it be your family? Your health? Your money? Your friends? Your faith? What would it be for you? Consider carefully your answer and then write it below.

#1 KEEPER _____

What's Important About Success To You?

We are going to examine one more priority. This is going to require an assistant to ask you these questions. This technique was taught in Bill Bachrach's High Trust Leadership Seminar, and in a book by the same name.[i] It is a tool used in sales to uncover core values in order to recommend proper investment options to match the client's heart objectives.

Have your assistant ask you these questions. As you answer each question, use your answer to the last one to complete the next question. It is crucial not to change the words of the core question even if it sounds a bit awkward. Also, have your assistant write the exact answers you give so they are able to ask the next question correctly.

(Answer #1 becomes question #2, etc. See my personal example below.)

What's important about success... to you?
_____

**What's important about (the above answer)_____
to you?**

**What's important about (the above answer)_____
to you?**

**What's important about (the above answer)_____
to you?***

Now, is there *anything* more important to you than your last answer? If so...keep going until you run out of answers.

As you progress through this exercise, it moves you from mind responses to heart ones. It uncovers your deeper, and then your deeper motivation, until you get to the heart of your life. It is like stripping away layers of an onion.

At Mr. Bacharach's seminar I discovered my personal core value, which enabled me to establish a personal mission statement. My answers are given below to demonstrate the effectiveness of this technique.

What's important about success... to you?
To be able to provide for my son.
What's important about being able to provide for your son to you?
I want to be able to give him more of the things in life that he wants.
What's important about being able to give him more of the things in life he wants to you?
It's important because after I provide for him, I can help others more.
What's important about helping others more to you?
I want to make a difference in people's lives— not just economically, but spiritually, emotionally, and any way that I can make a difference in lives.

When you arrive at your own core values, use your answer to write out a mission statement for your life.
My Mission Statement_____

When you uncover these "core values" be sure to pay attention to this need in your life. In your choice of careers, you will want to find a way to allow this "core value" to be expressed. When I was in business, my role as a financial planner made a difference in the lives of families I helped plan. As I moved past business into ministry, I had more opportunity to express that "core value". As I began to do seminars and guest speaking events to help people prioritize their lives and manage their time, I was making a difference. As I began to write books to inspire, teach, and motivate young people and children, again I found that satisfaction from doing what was deep inside my heart. I make a difference in lives. That makes my life worthwhile.

How about you? If your core value is security, then be sure to pursue a career with a steady paycheck and benefits that are dependable. A salesman who works on commission would not be the job for you. If your core value is being free to make your own choices, be sure to find a career that allows that freedom such as starting your own business. If your core value is helping others, perhaps the medical field would be appropriate. Do you see why it is important to know what moves your heart? Success isn't measured in dollars or awards, but in the fulfillment of the heart desire. As you define a mission statement for your own life, you will find that if you achieve *that purpose* you will have a sense of inward satisfaction.

With your mission statement in mind, analyze your present direction in life. Is there an avenue in your life to express your core value right now? How could you find a way to do it even as a teen?

What are your BIG ROCKS? (Priorities, Keeper, Core Value)

Take some time today to write a paper describing what you would like to do in life. Don't limit yourself. Let your imagination be free. Think a-bout what makes you feel satisfied and inner fulfillment. Think about your priorities. Consider your affections. What would a perfect life look like for you as an adult based on the things you have discovered about yourself?

*from Bill Bachrach's High Trust Leadership Seminars, © 1995 Bachrach & Associates, 8380 Miramar Mall Suite 233, Sand Diego CA 92121, 800-347-3707 Used by permission.

VI. CHANGE THE WORLD

QUOTE OF THE DAY
"The tissue of life to be
We weave with
colors all our own,
And in the
field of destiny
We reap
as we have sown".
John G. Whittier

VI. CHANGE THE WORLD

If you committed only 30 minutes per day to do SOMETHING positive for your community, you could make a huge impact on the world. In one year's time you would have spent 182 hours, 22 8-hour workdays, or the equivalent of $4\frac{1}{2}$ workweeks on it. Only 5 minutes, 3 times a day equals 92 hours in a year!

Little time commitments empowered by consistency bring great results! Set a specific time each day to work on your dream for your life.

Olympic winners are usually in their teens or early twenties. They did not get to the Olympics overnight! As a child, each one set his sights on a dream, began to practice, take lessons, focus his attention, and prioritize his life to see this dream become a reality. Olympians did not just wake up one day and decide they were really good and Olympic material. Greatness was formed through the years of sacrifice and commitment when no one was watching.

It is the little time commitment and consistency that keeps a dream alive in your heart and leads to greatness. Do you want to be great? There are a few suggestions to help you along on the next two pages.

- Schedule time in your planner and on your daily to do list for working on your dream.

- Schedule in quiet time each day to recharge.

- Writing it down makes you 30 % more likely to achieve it! Make a poster of your dream to look at often. Whether it is to be a professional dancer, athlete, or Miss America, find someone who is living your dream and use that to inspire you to do what it takes now to obtain greatness.

- Use your imagination! Once Miss America was asked how it felt to walk down the runway as she accepted the crown for winning the contest. She said it didn't make her nervous at all because she had walked down the aisle in her imagination thousands of times as a child.

- Get help! Teachers, parents, coaches, pastors, can all get behind you to encourage your dream.

- Work hard when no one else is looking.

- Consider your dream as you make choices all through life. If you want to be an athlete, you will have to take good care of your body. Drugs, cigarettes, or alcohol could spoil your pursuit of greatness in sports no matter how talented you may be.

- Don't give up! Keep on keeping on, one day at a time until you see it become reality.

- It takes 21 days to form a habit! Make a habit of taking the time to do what matters!

You *can* achieve greatness! You *can* change the world! Do it 30 minutes at a time!

Take a minute to "Selah"-
or stop and think about it.

How are *you* going to change the world?
What great thing
would you like to accomplish?

_____

_____

_____

_____

_____

_____

_____

_____

_____

_____

Community Projects

Do some research online or call the community center in your city to find out what opportunities available to serve in your community.

Some ideas:
- Serve at a soup kitchen
- Pick up trash at a park
- Volunteer at your library
- Read to a pre-school group
- Help an elderly neighbor or sick friend: rake their leaves, sweep their porch, shovel snow on their drive
- Take a homecooked meal to a shut-in.

There are endless possibilities of things you can do to help in your city!

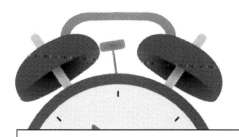

QUOTE OF THE DAY

"Help me to live each day
in such a way
that I accomplish
at least one thing
that will outlive me
and last for eternity."
Vernon Brewer

Put in the Big Rocks

Maybe your time is already filled up. How do you make time for everything? Try this experiment I found on the web to see what answers you conclude.

One day, an expert in time management was speaking to a group of business students and, to drive home a point, used an illustration those students will never forget. As he stood in front of the group of high-powered overachievers, he said, "Okay, time for a quiz." He pulled out a one gallon, 'wide-mouth' Mason jar and set it on the table in front of him. Then, he produced about a dozen fist sized rocks and carefully placed them, one by one, into the jar. When the jar was filled to the top and no more rocks would fit inside, he asked, "Is this jar full?" Everyone in the class said, "Yes."

Experiment
(Gather some fist sized rocks and borrow a jar or pitcher from your mom for this experiment. You can also use potatoes or styrofoam balls. Do this part of the experiment before reading further.)

He said, "Really?" He reached under the table and pulled out a bucket of gravel. Then he dumped some of the gravel in and shook the jar, causing pieces of gravel to work themselves down into the space between the big rocks.

Experiment part 2

Find some gravel if you used big rocks, or smaller styrofoam balls with styrofoam, or radishes with potatoes and work them into your pitcher or jar.

He asked the class once more, "Is this jar full?" By this time the class was on to him. "Probably not," one of them answered. "Good!" he replied.

He reached under the table and brought out a bucket of sand. He started dumping the sand into the jar and it went into all the spaces left between the rocks and the gravel.

Experiment part 3

For this part sand, sugar, or tiny styrofoam beads will do. Find some and pour it in.

Once more he asked the question, "Is this jar full?" "No!" the class shouted. Once again, he said, "Good!" Then he grabbed a pitcher of water and began to pour it in until the jar was filled to the brim.

> ## Experiment part 4
> Now pour some water into the jar, if you want to make a really big mess.

Then the expert in time management looked at the class and asked, "What is the point of this illustration?"

This is your assignment today. Do this experiment for yourself. What did this experiment show you? (Look for the answer on the next page after you have examined all your possibilities.)

_____

_____

_____

_____

_____

_____

_____

_____

_____

_____

A Skiers Dream

2010 Olympian Alpine Ski Team member, Lindsey Vann, had a dream. She said that as a little girl she always dreamed of being a great skier. Today, at 25, she is the top ranked American skier in the world.

How did this happen? It started as a child with a dream.. She added years of practice, hard work, and proper training. She was on skis by the time she was two. She began taking lessons and worked hard as a child. She was the first 11-14 year old American to win at Italy's Trofeo Troplini. By 18, she was a World Cup Champion.

Recently, I saw her Olympics ad and she said, "I didn't go to the prom" but she did not care. No doubt, she was too busy making a place in history for Lindsey Vann.

Perhaps you did not start as a child doing something, so you wonder how you can be great now. I was twenty-seven before I got the wake up call to start using my time wisely. I may have had a slower start, but I plan to have a great finish and enjoy the ride along the way! You can, too! Find your unique talent, work hard, and persevere!

Information from Wikipedia free online encyclopedia

QUIZ 3
CHANGE THE WORLD

1. 182 hours a year is only ___ minutes of work per day. 92 hour a year is only___ minutes ___ time a day.

2. It takes _____ to form a new habit.

3. _____ time commitments, empowered by _____ brings great results!

4. Why should you make a poster to look at of your dream or goal?

5. What does "selah" mean?

6. Why do you think it would help you as a child to think about what you want to accomplish in life now instead of later in life?

Big Rocks answer: If you don't put in the big rocks first, you can't fit them in at all!

BE A GOOD FINISHER

"The average person goes to his grave with his music still inside him." Zig Ziglar

Will YOU??? I know you are young, but we are going to do a what if?? Hopefully, this lesson will stick with you throughout life as you consider your path and help you make wise decisions. This assignment starts at the end of your life. If this were your last day alive, would you hold any regrets? If you continue living as you do now, when you come to the end of your earthly years, will you be satisfied that they have been spent well? Take a few minutes to answer the following questions. Are you on the path that will accomplish the things you hope to do with your life?

- Before I die, who do I want to be?

_____

_____

_____

_____

- Before I die, whom do I want to influence?

_____

_____

_____

_____

- Before I die, how do I want to be used?

_____

_____

_____

_____

- Before I die, what do I want people to say about me?

_____

_____

_____

_____

- What are my dreams and goals for 3-5 years from now and what am I doing today to make them a reality?

_____

_____

_____

_____

_____

_____

_____

_____

_____

As you think about changing the world, you will do it through something unique to you. Today is a good place to begin to live in greatness.

- What am I naturally good at doing?

  _____
  _____
  _____
  _____

- What do I really enjoy doing as a child?

  _____
  _____
  _____
  _____

- How am I going to be who and what I want to be in life?

  _____
  _____
  _____
  _____
  _____
  _____
  _____
  _____
  _____

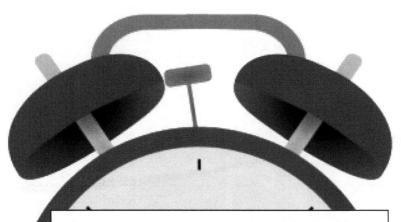

QUOTE OF THE DAY
"Sow an act,
and you reap a habit.
Sow a habit
and you reap a character.
Sow a character
and you reap a destiny."
Charles Reade

3 Things to Remember in a Race

1. Keep your eyes on the finish line

2. Don't look to see what the guy next to you is doing

3. Even when you can't go on- FINISH the race!

With clearly defined goals and a TO DO List in hand, if you learn to say NO to distracting things, you can do the GREAT things. Also, be careful to not step on others as you climb the ladder of success. Zig Ziglar, an expert in business success, said there are six things that are foundational to success: honesty, character, faith, integrity, love, and loyalty. Take a few minutes to look up each of these words in a dictionary.

Think about how you might develop these kinds of qualities. On a scale of 1 to 10, 10 being the best, how much of these foundational qualities to do you show in your life?

If you will apply just 30 minutes per day to seeing that big dream come true and do it the right way- in 1 year you will have spent the equivalent of 22- 8 hour workdays on it. You'll be on a path to real success!

VII. POWER TIME

QUOTE OF THE DAY
"In life, as in chess,
forethought wins."
Charles Buxton

MAKE A GRAPH

Estimate how long you spend on the main areas of your life: sleep, school, play, TV, family chores, etc. in a week.

Measure a piece of paper 168 inches (or cm)

Draw a rectangle on the page between the two points.

Next, measure each area and divide up your rectangle into class, sleep, eating, etc segments using each inch as an hour.

Color each segment.

This is what you did with your TIME this week.

Analyze your time usage. Are there areas that need to be adjusted?

VII. MY POWER TIME

How can you do your work well each and every day? Besides developing the character to do things right, another important factor is to learn to manage your time. One important factor in your being productive (the ability to get things done) is to plan around your natural body clock strengths. Think about these questions to find out, "What is my POWER TIME?" Am I an early bird? A night owl? Or an afternoon snoozer? A key to success is to plan your most *demanding* jobs during your strength times.

1. What time of the day do you feel most productive?

2. What time do you feel mentally alert?

3. What time do you have trouble concentrating?

4. What time do you feel tired or burned out?

5. When do you exercise, pursue hobbies or sports?

6. What time do you want to go to bed?

7. When do you wake up (without an alarm)?

8. Are you a cheerful "morning person"?

How Does this Apply to You?

Looking at the answers on the last page:
When do you think you should you do homework?

When should you plan time to veg or watch TV?

When should you plan to study for a test?

When should you schedule an important meeting?

Should you stay up late or get up early to be most productive?

Talk with your parents about these things. If it is easier to learn early in the day, use that time for high concentration assignments. Schedule your harder classes during your peak productivity. Schedule easier tasks in your weaker times. You will accomplish more during your peak performance times and finish it more quickly.

If you are a morning person and feel worn out in the evening when it is time to do homework, consider a power nap to regain that morning vitality. Set an alarm for 30 minutes just after school for a brief nap. You will wake up with new energy, fresh to complete the work. Be sure not to nap long or take it too late in the evening. That may interfere with going to sleep at night.

VIII. A BUSY GENERATION

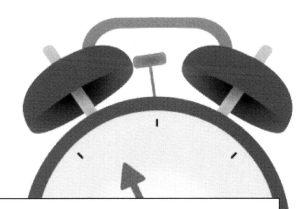

QUOTE OF THE DAY
"How pleasant it is at the
end of the day,
no follies to have to
repent,
But reflect on the past,
and be able to say
That my time has been
properly spent!"
Jane Taylor

VIII. A BUSY GENERATION

As we said before, you have access to more activities than any generation before. This is why you need to learn skills to control your time more than any previous generation.

NOTE: A "generation" is a group of people about the same age, like you, your friends, and your brothers and sisters are part of a generation. Your parents and people their age are a generation and your grandparents make up a generation.

Life is more fast-paced than in your parent's generation. Everything is getting faster! New technology gives your generation access to more information than earlier generations. That speeded up society also gives your generation more opportunity to be overloaded and stressed at a younger age. This is why you need to learn skills to control and manage your time more than any previous generation.

RESEARCH ASSIGNMENT

Interview your parents and see what life was like as a teenager. What games did they play as children and teens? Did they have internet? How fast or slow was it? Did they have cell phones? Video games? What was school like for your parents? When were they expected to be able to read, add and subtract, etc. Did they feel stressed? Does their childhood sound boring? Why?

Call your grandparents and ask about their childhood. If you could choose, which generation would you prefer to live as a teenager?

☐ My grandparents   ☐ My parents   ☐ My generation

What I found out about life in my parents and grandparents childhood and teenage life:

_____

_____

_____

_____

_____

_____

_____

_____

TIME TO "PLAY"

Whether you are 6 or 16, you need time each day that is not scheduled with activity. You NEED down time. That is time to just do whatever you want or "unstructured time." You need time to daydream and use your imagination. Be careful planning too many outside activities. You need to be at home to just relax at least two nights a week. Do you have free time? Make the following graph to see how much time you have for yourself:

Create a graph with the days of the week across the top of the page and each of the 24 hours down the side. Color in all the things you do have to do every day: sports, music, school, chores, mealtime, family obligations, church, homework. Use estimated time for this one.

Color in the time you spend doing each task. Add the time you sleep to the top of the graph. Now, see how much time is left over. Out of this time, block off time for playing with friends or other unplanned activity. Be sure to save time to daydream as well. Children and teens are experiencing stress related illnesses at an alarming rate. Planning "Down Time" can help make your life more balanced and reduce stress.

TIME GRAPH

	Su	Mo	Tu	We	Th	Fr	Sa
1AM							
2A							
3A							
4A							
5A							
6A							
7A							
8A							
9A							
10A							
11A							
12A							
1PM							
2P							
3P							
4P							
5P							
6P							
7P							
8P							
9P							
10P							
11P							
12P							

QUIZ 4

1. What is a generation?

2. Why do you think your generation is busier?

3. What is a POWER TIME?

"History will be kind to me For I intend to write it." **Winston Churchhill**

IX. THE HISTORY OF TIME MANAGEMENT

QUOTE OF THE DAY
"Cling to the flying hours;
and yet
Let one pure hope,
one great desire,
Like song on dying lips, be set, --
That ere we fall in scattered fire,
Our hearts may lift the world's
heart higher."
Edmund W. Gosse

IX.
THE HISTORY OF
TIME MANAGEMENT

"Chronos" is the ancient word for time that refers to the measurement of the passage of our days and years. We use clocks and calendars to measure time.

Tools to measure time were first used about 3500 B.C. Day and night was easy to identify (except if you lived in the Arctic tundra where the sun doesn't go down and doesn't come up sometimes.) Take some time today to study about the days in the Arctic. Find out why their days are so long and short. Write an imaginary story about life in the land of the Midnight sun.

For most of us, the sun comes up in the morning and goes down at night, making one day. At first, people would simply tell time by the sun. When it was directly overhead, it was the middle of the day, or noon. When it was on the horizon it was either morning (sunrise) or evening (sunset). Telling time this way was not very accurate.

MEASURING TIME

Before there were clocks, how did teenagers get to school at a specific time? How did people know what time it was? Today, we use clocks to tell us the time of day. The work "clock" was first used about 700 years ago. It comes from a Latin word for bell, "Clocca".

Ancient civilizations used hourglasses, sundials, and water clocks to measure the passing of time.

'Obelisks' (tall four-sided tapered monuments) were built around 3500 BC. (about 5,500 years ago) to measure the shadow cast by the sun. It was marked into sections that divided the day into two halves.

Around 1500 B.C. ancient Egyptians created a 'shadow clock' or 'sundial'.

It measured the passage of hours. The circle was divided into ten parts, with two 'twilight hours' for morning and evening. The shadow of the sun pointed to a number on the circular disk that showed the time. At midday, the device had to be turned 180 degrees to measure the afternoon hours.

HOURGLASSES, WATER CLOCKS, AND MERKHETS

Hourglasses were invented at Alexandria about the middle of the third century. People carried them around like we carry a watch today. An hourglass consists of two glass bulbs filled with fine sand which flows through a narrow tube at a given rate, usually one hour.

About 1400 B.C. (about 3,400 years ago), the Egyptians invented a water clock. It was called a "clepsydra." A water clock was made of two containers of water. One was higher than the other. Water traveled through a tube from the higher to the lower container. The container had marks to show the water level. The marks told the time. Water clocks told the time even at night.

Around 600 B.C. (about 2,600 years ago), the Egyptians made a tool to study the stars that also told the time at night. It was called a 'Merkhet' and is the oldest known astronomical tool. Two merkhets were used to find a north-south line by lining them up with the 'Pole Star'. By observing when certain stars crossed the marked meridian, they could measure hours at night as well.

The Egyptians and Babylonians divided the day from sunrise to sunset into twelve parts that were called hours. They also divided the night into twelve parts, from sunset to sunrise. The problem was, the day and night are not the same length, and the length of a day changes through the year.

Finally, someone decided it was better to divide the entire day/night into 24 hours of equal length. This way time could be measured more accurately.

The hour is divided into 60 minutes and each minute is divided into 60 seconds. The idea to divide time into 60 parts came from the Sumerian sexagesimal system, based on the number 60, which was developed about 4,000 years ago.

QUOTE OF THE DAY
"The passing minute is everyman's equal possession, but what has once gone by is not ours."
Marcus Aurelius

MAKE A SUNDIAL

Take some time this week to study how sundials work. Make your very own sundial.

The following link shows an easy instruction guide for your own "sun clock".

You will need a compass and stopwatch for this project.

www.exploratorium.edu/scie nce_explorer/sunclock.html

QUIZ 5
TIME HISTORY

1. (Chronos or Kairos) is the way we measure time by calendars and clocks.

2. Tools to measure time were first used in _____ B.C.

3. What were obelisks?

4. How does a sundial work?

5. Name two ways the Eqyptians measured time at night.

CALENDARS

Where did we get the calendar? The Greeks divided the year into twelve parts that are called months. Their year had a total of 360 days, or 12 times 30 (12x30=360). Since the earth goes around the Sun in one year and follows almost a circular path, they decided to divide the circle into 360 degrees.

The year is 364 days, 5 hours, 48 minutes, 46 seconds long or 364.242199 days. All calendars started with people recording time using things in nature. They used day and night, cycles of the moon or lunar cycles, and cycles of the sun or solar cycles to set a pattern of predictable time.

The time between full moons is 29.53 days. People attempted to keep track of time by the moon cycles, but there was a problem. The lunar cycle did not divide evenly. A month (moon-th) measured by the moon did not give an equal number of days. A solar year did not equal a certain number of moon cycles.

Some people would line up calendars to the moon cycle, making some months 29 days and others 30.

Others, like the Jewish and Chinese calendar, made special rules and added "leap months" some years to line up with the sun's cycle.

The LUNAR calendar used the moon to track time.

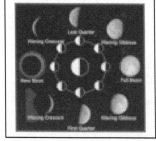

The calendar that used the sun to track time was called the SOLAR calendar.

What problems do you see in having a calendar that changes every year?_____

_____

_____

_____

_____

EXPERIMENT
Study the moon cycle. Make a calendar based on lunar days. Start each month on a full moon.

THE FIRST CALENDARS

The Ancient Egyptians made the first 12-month calendar. They made each month an even 30 days, adding 5 days at the end of the year to line up with the solar year. Greek rulers of Egypt under Ptolemy added the leap year concept, adding a day every 4 years.

We got the idea of a different number of days each month from the Romans. Their early calendar was 12 months, beginning in March. Later January became the start of the year.

The early Romans tried to line up the months with the first crescent moon each month. This made some months 29 days, and others 31 with a leap year concept. The problem was that over four years, the calendar was off 4 days to the solar cycle.

Finally, Julius Caesar asked an astronomer, Sosigenes of Alexandria, to make a better calendar. He created the Julian calendar. He made some months 30 days, some 31, adding an extra day in February in leap years.

The first day of each month was called "Kalendae" or calends. Debts were due on this day each month. This is where we got the term "calendar."

You probably learned this little verse as a child: *"Thirty days has September, April, June, and November, all the rest have 31, except February that has 28 until leap year gives it 29."*
Author unknown

Leap years were added to balance the ¼ day left over each year. Leap year day is also a great day to evaluate your goals and plans.

When was the last leap year?_____

Take some time today to describe what you were doing in the last leap year. How old were you? Your family? What pets did you have? What grade were you in? Where did you live? Did you have any long range plans? What did you think you would have done by now that you haven't?

When is the next leap year?_____

Jot down some things you would like to accomplish before the next leap year. How will you ensure you will accomplish these plans or goals?

Contemplate Your Life

Have you ever thought about this question: "What do I want to accomplish in this lifetime?" Often we make lists of those things, but year after year there is no real sense of getting even one step closer to those heart dreams. How do we change that never-ending cycle of not getting "around to it"?

Draw a big circle with hour marks but no numbers. Put a "0" at the top where the 12 number would be and draw the big hand of the clock there. Estimate your life span in years. Put that number in the space just left of your "0", indicating the end of your life. Now, estimate your position on the clock according to your current age and draw the small hand of the clock there. That now separates your past from your future.

Take a few minutes to list out the things in your past you want to be remembered for, special treasured moments, and things you have done to get to the dream in your heart so far.

Now, divide the remaining future time into 4-year "leap year" increments, starting with the last leap year. Take careful thought of each step along the path of your future. Pencil into the correct year things you already can estimate, such as when you will go to college, graduate, or pay off your car.

Finally, set specific goals for each four-year period to make steps toward completing all you desire to do and be in life. Each leap year, take an account of your progress. It is easy to remember because you can do this on February 29th.

Take an account of what has been accomplished in that four-year time frame. How much have you matured over those four years? How has your relationships and family life improved from four years ago? Have you lost or gained weight? Have you gone on that vacation or mission trip you keep planning to do "someday"? Do you see the four years well invested, or four years of simply existing?

Now, set specific goals for the next four years. Put $\frac{1}{4}$ of those goals on your yearly agenda, and daily do something to achieve them. If it is only 15 minutes a day, over the course of 4 years that will accumulate into 364 1/4 hours. How many days are in a year? 364 $\frac{1}{4}$. Isn't that interesting?

WHAT ABOUT A.D. and B.C.

In early history, people counted the years by the reign of the Roman emperor or by the Bible, calculating time since Adam.

Dionysius set the year to 0 at Jesus Christ's incarnation (the nativity) based on historic information available to him. This became the time line point of reference for measuring years.

The term A.D. (Anno Donimi-in the year of Our Lord) was not introduced until the 6th century by the monk Dionysius Exiguus.   The term B.C. (Before Christ) refers to the time preceding this event.

QUIZ 6
CALENDARS

1. How long is a year?

2. Why did the "moon cycle" calendar not work well?

3. Who made the first twelve-month calendar?

4. What was the Julian calendar?

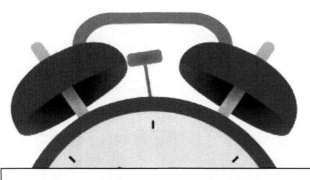

QUOTE OF THE DAY
"History is a mighty drama,
enacted upon
the theatre of time,
with suns for lamps,
and eternity for a
background."
Thomas Carlyle

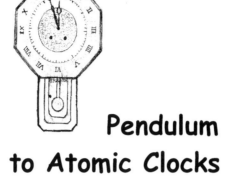

Pendulum to Atomic Clocks

Peter Henlein of Germany invented a spring-powered clock about 1510. It was not very accurate. The first clock with a minute hand was invented by Jost Burgi in 1577. It also did not work very well. The first practical clock was the pendulum clock. It was developed in 1656 by Christan Huygens. By 1600, a minute hand was added.

The pendulum swings left and right, and as it swings, it turns a wheel with teeth. The turning wheel turns the hours and minutes on the clock face. The pendulum would stop swinging after a while and have to be restarted. In 1840, battery operated pendulum clocks were introduced. Their batteries were on the outside of the clock. In 1906, the battery was moved inside the clock.

In 1920, very precise Quartz clocks were invented. Quartz is a type of crystal that looks like glass. When you apply electricity and pressure, the quartz vibrates at a very constant rate. This vibration moved the clock hands very precisely.

Though alarm triggers on clocks date back to Plato in (428-348 B.C.) who had an alarm on his water clock, the first mechanical clock as we know it was invented by Levi Hutchus of New Hampshire in the US. He made it for himself and it only rang at 4 A.M. to get him up for work. The French inventor, Antoine Redier, was the first to patent an adjustable mechanical clock in 1847.

The atomic clock was invented by the English inventor, Louise Essen, in the 1950s. It uses the energy changes that take place in an atom to keep track of time. Atomic clocks are so accurate they only lose 1 second every 2 to 3 million years.

Abbreviations for TIME

second - sec.
minute - min.
hour - hr.
week - wk.
month - mo.
year - yr.

ante meridiem
(before noon) - a.m.

post meridiem
(after noon) - p.m.

midnight - 12:00 a.m.
noon - 12:00 p.m.

MAKE AN HOURGLASS

Wash and dry two empty soft drink 16 oz bottles. Fill one with sand, salt, or sugar. Tape a second bottle on top of the full one.

Turn the bottle over and use a stopwatch to see how many seconds it takes to empty the bottle.

Calculate how many times you would have to invert the bottle immediately after it is empty to time 1 HOUR.

———

Set a timer for 1 HOUR and test your experiment.

Were your calculations close?

QUOTE OF THE DAY
"Don't waste your life in
doubts and fears:
spend yourself on the work
before you,
well assured that
the right performance
of this hour's duties
will be the best preparation
for the hours and ages
that follow it."
Ralph Waldo Emerson

TIME ZONES

Before the 1900s, people set their clocks by the sun, causing time to be different in different towns across America. The railroads changed all that. They instituted STANDARD TIME so everyone was on the same time system. Standard time is the time that is established by law for a country or city. The concept was born to avoid confusion in the train system that was caused by each town using its solar time.

The railroad system needed to be "time" precise. Every railroad engineer had an officially tested and approved pocket watch that had to be checked regularly to keep the trains running according to a strict time schedule. A second late or early could mean crashing with another train!

Sir Sandford Fleming, a Canadian railroad planner, devised the plan for worldwide standard time in the 1870s. It is basically the same one in place today. There are 24 standard meridians of longitude (lines running from the North Pole to the South) 15 degrees apart which indicate the 24 time zones.

The railroads brought a new "time" awareness to Americans. They began to keep schedules and became conscious of "being on time" which caused businesses to prosper.

QUOTE OF THE DAY
"First comes thought;
then organization of that
thought into ideas and plans;
then transformation of those
plans into reality.
The beginning, as you will
observe,
is in your imagination."
Napoleon Hill

X.
TIME
RESPONSIBILITY

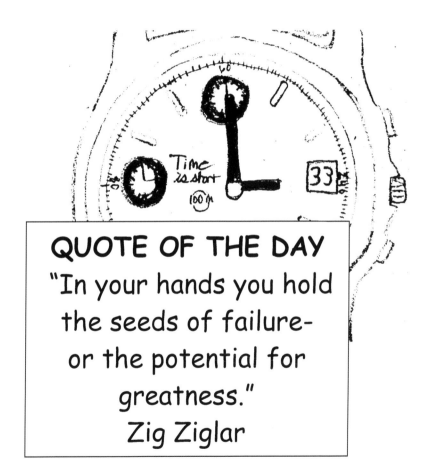

QUOTE OF THE DAY
"In your hands you hold
the seeds of failure-
or the potential for
greatness."
Zig Ziglar

X.
TIME RESPONSIBILITY

Each morning you receive 24 hours or 86,400 seconds in your TIME BANK. What you do with those seconds is what shapes your life. Every night while you are sleeping, your time bank gets zeroed.

You cannot carry minutes forward and use them tomorrow. You cannot borrow time from yesterday. You do not get interest on minutes you don't use. Instead your account returns to 86,400 again the next morning and you begin spending from your time account the moment you open your eyes all over again.

How many minutes do you have each day?_____

Where are your minutes are going:
1. Where do you spend most of your free time?

_____
_____
_____

2. Do you ever feel like you don't have enough time?

_____
_____

3. How have you noticed time seeming to speed up or slow down? Have you noticed how long it seems when you are waiting and how short your visit with your best friend seems to be?

_____

_____

_____

4. How much time do you spend watching television, playing video games, on the internet, texting? (The average youth spends 1.7-3 hours watching TV, 3-5 hours on the internet, and texts 80 times daily)

_____

_____

_____

5. What jobs do you do to help your family? How much time do you spend doing your jobs each day?

_____

_____

_____

6. In how many outside activities do you participate? (Youth group, dance, sports, swimming, scouts, etc.) How much time per week do you spend doing all these activities (include driving time)?

_____

_____

_____

7. If you never had to go to school or help around the house, what would you do with your time?

_____

_____

_____

8. If you never had to work when you grow up, what would you like to be able to do everyday?

_____

_____

_____

9. What do you wish your parents had more time to do?

_____

_____

Spend some time today discussing your schedule with your parents. If there are activities you would like to add, it would be a good time to talk about that. If you are going to a sport or meeting that you really do not enjoy, talk about that, too.

EXPERIMENT
Keep a log each time you watch TV,
play video games, are on the computer,
text or talk on the phone.
Add it up at the end of the week.
Does it surprise you?

Weed Your Time Garden

All that unproductive "Stuff" that fills your time are like WEEDS! They choke the life out of your day. Weeds use up all the nutrients in the soil of your time that that should be directed toward growing things to make you GREAT!

Your generation has more distractions than any in the past. TV, internet, phones, ipods, or video games are not the problem. The problem is not having any vision or purpose for your life today.

Statistics show the average high school student has watched over 18,000 hours of TV over his school years. The average teen spends 2- 3 hours of TV daily, 3 average hours on the internet, and time texting 80 times a day, which may account for much of your time.

This generation has to seriously learn to steward their time. If not, all the convenience and fun things will consume all your time so there is nothing left. If they are managed with wisdom, they can be a source of relaxation and fun.

Years ago, I decided I was tired of watching other people live out their dreams and decided to turn my TV watching time into making my dreams a reality! I turned off the TV, watching only choice things, and began using the time for creativity and family. If I had continued in my habit of watching TV in my free time, I might never have had the time to give inspiration and creativity a place to work.

List some things you don't have time to do.

_____

_____

_____

_____

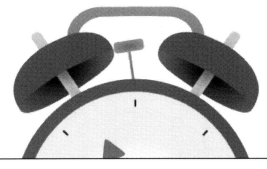

QUOTE OF THE DAY
"Anyone who does not believe in himself and fully utilize his ability is literally stealing from himself."
Zig Ziglar

WHERE IS YOUR TIME GOING?

- How many times a day do you complain, worry, gripe?_____

- Estimate the time you spend thinking about problems each day._____

- How much time a day do you spend daydreaming?_____
(The average person spends 1/3 of their time)

- How many hours a day do you spend watching television? _____
Now, multiply that by 7 for a week_____

- How many hours a day do you spend playing video games?_____
Now multiply that by 7 for a week _____

- How many hours do you spend text messaging/ on the phone?_____
Now multiply that by 7 for a week_____

- How many hours do you spend on the internet?_____
Now multiply that by 7 for a week_____

Add up all the subtotals from the previous page
_____

There are 168 hours in a week-
8 daily for sleep leaves 112 hours waking hours.

What percentage of YOUR time is potentially weeds
per week?_____
(Look on the last page and add up a week)

11 hours (about 1.5 hours a day)=10% of waking hrs.

22 hours (about 3 hours a day) is 20%,

33 hours (about 4.5 hours a day) is 30% of your
time awake.

QUOTE OF THE DAY
"I wasted time, and now time
doth wasted me."
William Shakespeare

KEEPING A TIME LOG

This week you will be watching how you use your time very carefully.

1. Copy the TIME LOG on the next page.

2. Keep it with you all day for an entire week.

3. Record each thing you do throughout the day.
    What time did you go to bed?
    What time did you get up?
    How much time did you spend at soccer?
    How long did you work on chores?

4. At the end of the week, color each square the color of what you were doing.

5. Evaluate your week.
How balanced is your life?
Do you have plenty of all the colors?
Are there areas that need to be adjusted?

My Time Log

	MON.	TUE.	WED.	THR.	FRI.	SAT.	SUN.
7 A.M.							
8 A.M.							
9 A.M.							
10 A.M.							
11 A.M.							
12 P.M.							
1 P.M.							
2 P.M.							
3 P.M.							
4 P.M.							
5 P.M.							
6 P.M.							
7 P.M.							
8 P.M.							
9 P.M.							
10 P.M.							
11 P.M.							
12 A.M.							
1 A.M.							
2 A.M.							
3 A.M.							
4 A.M.							
5 A.M.							
6 A.M.							

Quiet Time(blue)   TV/Internet (black)
Family (yellow)   Social Life/friends/texting (orange)
Sleep (green)   Charitable/church meetings (brown)
School(red)   Hobbies/recreation (purple)

QUIZ 7
Time Bank

1. Every morning you receive _____ seconds into your time bank.

2. The average youth spends _____ watching TV daily and
   _____ on the internet daily.

3. What's an objective?

4. How does an hourglass work?

5. What is a time log?

XI.
ORGANIZATION

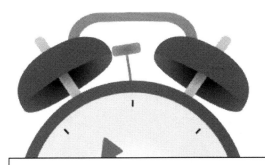

QUOTE OF THE DAY
"Trust no future
howe'er pleasant;
Let the dead past
bury its dead;
Act,—act in the living present,
Heart within
and God o'erhead!"
Henry Wadsworth Longfellow

XI. ORGANIZATION

One of the biggest time wasters is not being able to find something you need or want. Having all your equipment in one place and in operating order will make homework time shorter. If you can't find a pencil, you have to stop and dig through your backpack for one. Then, it needs sharpening and you can't find the pencil sharpener. That takes more time. You get started on the assignment and realize you need the dictionary to look up something and can't find it. Again, you lose more time searching. You can spend as much time looking for what you need FOR your homework as you spend ON your homework!

This week, take some time to organize your life: your desk or locker at school, your room, your study area at home, and your closet. You will be SO glad that you did!

1. Assign a place for everything. Half the battle is won when we just have a specific place to always put things! When you finish using something put it back in its place!

2. Make a TO DO, TO READ, TO FILE folders. When you get assignments, reading projects, or papers that need to file for semester tests; sort

them immediately and put in the proper folder. Sort them by subject. Carry your TO DO and TO READ file with you for waiting times. Fifteen (15) minutes per day = 92 hours per year! You will be surprised at how many waiting minutes you have in a week that could be productive!

3. Anything empty, ripped, the wrong size or not worn, new or used, put in the trash or a charity box immediately. Don't just reshuffle it.

4. Put things where they work for you: vitamins beside juice glasses, coat hooks in the garage next to the car, a drawer or box for school supplies beside where you do homework, etc.

5. Use Baskets. They clean up clutter. Use a shoe basket by the door so you can always find shoes (and those of little brothers and sisters that make you late because they can't find them.) Put an "OUTGOING" basket by the front door for anything that needs to go out next trip— library books or movies to return, letters to mail, notes for school, etc. Use a small basket for all your remotes beside the bed and on an end table in the den. A basket beside a power strip is a great place for all the unplugged remotes from phones, ipods, video recorders, etc. Never lose

your charger again, and save some energy this way as well.

6. Use clear plastic containers in your closet to sort all the things that are alike together. Clearly label them on the outside. You can use boxes with labels as well.

7. Use under the bed storage area if you need extra storage.

8. Sort the clothes in your closet, long sleeve, short sleeve shirts, jeans in a section, dress clothes in a section to make finding the right thing to wear easier.

9. Make separate drawers or section off a drawer for socks, underwear, etc.

10. Use a cork bulletin board in your room for all the little special things you want to save—a recital program, ticket stubs from a concert, random pictures of your friends.

11. As you help with household chores, use a plastic rectangular basket with handles loaded with paper towels, a dust cloth, bath, toilet, and glass and furniture cleaner. Carry it room to room.

12. Put a liner in the wastebasket in every room. (Store new folded ones under the one in use). When you notice the trash full in your room, it is easy to pick up as you are carrying other things.

13. Baskets in the garage keep all your car cleaning materials in one place. Baskets for basketballs, soccer equipment, etc. also keep everything in one place.

STOP WASTING TIME!

When your teacher or parents tell you to stop wasting time, what are they really saying? What they mean is that you are not using your time in the right way.

If a fish were swimming in the ocean, would you tell it to stop wasting water? Of course not! Water is all around. The fish just swims in it.

In the same way, you cannot really "waste time." You are swimming in "time" just like a fish in water. It is all around you. What you are really wasting is *yourself*. In this course, I want to help teach you to do a better job with your time. You and your talents are too important to waste.

Time is valuable. Your parents are paid for the time they are on the job. Can you think of ways you might be wasting your time?

QUOTE OF THE DAY

"Don't waste your life in doubts and fears: spend yourself on the work before you, well assured that the right performance of this hour's duties will be the best preparation for the hours and ages that follow it."

Ralph Waldo Emerson

TIME IS MONEY

Many jobs pay on a "commission" basis. That means a person is paid for the work they perform, or sales they make, not the number of hours they work. For these people, learning to use their TIME wisely is very important.

An hourly employee can also cost a company a tremendous amount of money when he is not time conscious. Do you know how much it would cost a company in the course of a year if an employee wasted only 60 minutes per day? (That is four 15-minute personal calls or trips to the coffee machine.)

If the employee was paid $25 per hour, or $52,000 in a year, 60 minutes per day lost to distractions, personal pursuits, wasted time at the coffee machine, etc. would cost a company $6,500 in a year.

Calculate what an hour lost each day would cost at $10 per hour in a year. (40 hr. work week/52 weeks)

What is the minimum wage rate? This is the rate most teens begin work. What would it cost your employer if you wasted an hour each day?

EXPERIMENT

This week, make a box for each area of your life: sleep, school, family time, exercise, TV/Video games, phone, computer, sports, and wasted time. Start your week with 168 dimes. Each time you spend an hour, put in a dime. At the end of your week, see how much time you are "spending" on wasted time.

QUOTE OF THE DAY
"A penny saved
is a penny earned."
Benjamin Franklin

SET A DEADLINE!

If you were asked to clean out your closet this Saturday, how long would it take to complete the job? Probably all day.

If you were going out with friends at 1 PM and had to have your closet cleaned out before you left, how long would it take you? Until about 12:30?

Does having a time limit on a job help you to stay focused?

Do you work faster knowing it had to be done on time?

Experiment with this concept this week. See how long it takes to do a job without any time limits.

Then, do the same job using a timer, or a limit of time to complete the job. Which way was faster?

Why do you think your parents go to work for 8 hours a day instead of just doing it whenever they feel like it?

I FORGOT!

You are busy! With school, friends, sports, family, church, dance and everything else you do, you have so many things to keep up with and do! How do you expect to remember it all? You need ways to jog your memory to accomplish everything!

1. **To DO Lists**- Keep a notepad handy to jot down things you need to do and give your memory a break! A simple TO DO List helps keep you on track throughout your day. Keep your list visible. I keep a tiny note pad in my car for this!

2. When you want to remember something but can't write it down, carry a tiny personal recorder or an ipod **to record thoughts**, things TO DO, songs, or GREAT ideas that pop into your head.

3. **Call and leave yourself a message!** If you have something you need to do when you get home, call home and leave yourself a message on the answering machine.

4. **Use an email reminder/text message service** for your parents to keep up with all that is going on at school, weather cancellations, etc.

5. **Visible calendar.** Keep a calendar where you see it every day. At the first of the year, transfer all your birthdays and important dates to the next year. When you have special events like a soccer match, practice, recital, or concert put them on your master calendar immediately. Record everyone's schedule such as dance lessons, soccer, etc in identifying colors on the calendar. Check your calendar each day as you prepare a TO DO List.

6. **Post stick it notes!** If you need to remember something before you leave the house, post a note on the inside of your front door. Have an urgent call in the morning? Put a post it note on your phone. Need to remember to pick up something on the way home, stick a note on the car dash and forget it until the end of the day.

7. **Use alarm clocks and timers.** Decide when you need to start getting ready for an event and set an alarm. You'll never get busy and forget guitar lessons or dance again! Set it for 15 minutes before you need to be out the door to get to school or practice so you are gearing toward getting out the door.

QUOTE OF THE DAY

When a secretary
of George Washington,
excusing himself
for being late,
said that his watch
was too slow,
the reply of Washington
was,
"You must get
a new watch,
or I must get
a new secretary."

What is Time?

"What I do today is important.
What I accomplish must be worthwhile
Because the price IS HIGH!"
Author Unknown

Time is a *natural resource* that is becoming like an endangered species. Nobody seems to have enough of it anymore! How many times have you wanted to go to shoot baskets or play x-box but needed to run a brother or sister to an event or your parents were busy? Your parents tell you, "We don't have time for that right now." What are some things that keep your parents busy?

_____
_____
_____
_____
_____
_____
_____
_____

It is very important to take time every day to talk with your parents. Ask if they will schedule time in their planner for you each and every day.

TIME IS AN ASSET

Time is a precious commodity that is given equally to each one of us. No one has a larger store than anyone else does.

Time can be an asset or a liability.
You can't borrow it
You can't earn more
You can't store it up
All you can do is spend it.

Look up the definition of asset and liability.
Which is time to you?

**Each day you receive 86,400 seconds
into your time bank.**

There are no forwarding balances.
There are no overdrafts.
Or interest accrued on seconds not used.

You lose it all at midnight and
each morning you get a fresh supply.

If you receive 86,400 seconds each day,
how many minutes do you have to spend each day?

If your minutes were dollars
would you spend them more carefully?

We can never "save" time; we can only spend it.
To tell someone not to waste time is like telling a fish in the ocean not to waste water.
Time is all around us.
You are wasting -YOURSELF.

Time problems are not from the <u>supply</u> of time- but rather the <u>use</u> of that time that determines the quality of your life and your productivity.

You don't "find" time— you "make" it. It is a proven fact that you WILL make time for what is truly important to you.

List some things you have "made" time for that were not in your regular schedule in the past month.

_____

_____

_____

You MAKE time when your favorite program is having a special hour long premier. You MAKE time when you have extra practices for the game or recital. You MAKE time when your best friend wants you to come over. What we SAY is important to us—and what REALLY IS important to us is revealed in how we spend our time.

QUIZ 8
A NATURAL RESOURCE

1. If you are paid $5 an hour, how long would you have to work to buy an IPOD Touch (average cost about $200)?

2. Describe why deadlines help you finish faster?

3. What is an asset?

4. Time is a _____ commodity.

5. We can never _____ time, we can only _____ it.

6. Time problems are not from the _____ of time, but rather the _____ of time.

QUOTE OF THE DAY
"The future is something
that everyone reaches
at the rate of
sixty minute an hour,
Whatever he does,
whoever he is."
C. S. Lewis

TIME PROBLEMS

We each have been given exactly the same amount of time—168 hours in a week.

How many minutes are in a day?

In a week?

How many seconds are in a day?

In a week?

No matter how you measure it, a week is the same length of time. That remains the same whether you are a little child, a teenager, a parent, or a grandparent. It is the same whether you are a basketball star or a little hungry child in Africa.

It is what we do with our time that determines how well we do at school, how happy we are, and whether we feel satisfied and relaxed or worried and anxious. In reality, time is what makes our life worthwhile.

This course is to help you want to learn how to use your time the right way. You are important to this world! Learning to steward (the way you use) your time and talents well will help you succeed in life.

MY DAILY TIME LOG

12 AM_____

1 AM_____

2 AM_____

3 AM_____

4 AM_____

5 AM_____

6 AM_____

7 AM_____

8 AM_____

9 AM_____

10 AM_____

11 AM_____

12 PM _____

1 PM_____

2 PM_____

3 PM_____

4 PM_____

5 PM_____

6 PM_____

7 PM_____

8 PM_____

9 PM_____

10 PM_____

11 PM_____

WHERE DOES YOUR TIME GO?

Make a list of all the things you need to do today. Estimate how long it takes to do each thing.

Example: School: 7 hours
Bath: 15 minutes
Eating: 1 hour
Chores: 1 hour
Driving to school and home: 30 minutes
Sports or activity: 1 hour (be sure to add time for getting ready, driving to lessons, and time to get things put away at home)
Sleep 8 hours
Add up all these numbers and subtract them from 24. That is how much FREE TIME you have today.

Let's keep an actual log of what you do with your day today, hour by hour, with the Daily Time Log. How did your estimated time to do things measure up to your real time log?

A "Budget" is a list of how much you spend compared to how much you earn. Budgets are used for household finances to determine where the money needs to go and how to have enough money for everything that needs to be paid. Today, we're going to do a TIME budget. Do you have enough time?

My Time "Budget"

Expenses:

Sleep _____ per week

School:

Classes _____ per week

Homework _____ per week

Total school time_____

Family Time

    Meals Together _____ per week

    Games/Activities_____ per week

    Devotions _____ per week

    Family Meeting _____ per week

Total family time_____

Friends

    Phone/Text Msg _____ per week

    Visiting _____ per week

Total friends time____

TV/Movies _____ per week

Video Games _____ per week

Internet _____ per week

Total screen time_____

Creative Arts	_____	per week
Music/Dance/etc.	_____	per week
Imagination time	_____	per week

Total entertainment time____

Exercise/playing outside_____		per week
Sports/Dance/hiking	_____	per week

Total exercise time_____

Church/Youth Group	_____	per week
Community Service	_____	per week

Total church/community time____

Personal
Showers/Hair/Grooming_____		per week
Eating	_____	per week
Quiet Time	_____	per week
Other_____	_____	per week

Total Personal time   ____

Total TIME expenses _____
TIME Income: 168 hours/ week

MY FREE CHOICE TIME _____

XII.
TEENS CAN DO
GREAT THINGS

QUOTE OF THE DAY
"If you don't know
where you are going,
you'll end up
someplace else."
Yogi Berra

XII. TEENS CAN
DO GREAT THINGS

Your generation stands on the brink of the most amazing time in history. You, as a generation, have the potential to radically change the course of history. You have dreams in your heart of changing the world. The question is— will you have TIME to do that?

That may sound silly right now, but have you noticed how quickly time is passing? As high school makes way to graduation and college, then you'll need to get that job and perhaps marry your college sweetheart. Then, children and career will further consume your time.

The next thing you know, twenty years have gone by and you are no closer to fulfilling the dreams in your heart than when you first started. That's the reason for TIME 4 HIGH SCHOOL. My goal is not ONLY for you to succeed at school, but to succeed at life. I want to help you to be great! I believe in your generation, and have faith it will be the greatest generation this world has ever known!

REALITY CHECK

College sounds so far away! Did you know that if you are a freshman in high school, you will be starting college 1,457 days?.

What you do with the rest of your life, and what you do before you get to college, will be decided <u>one</u> day at a time. How old are you? How many days do you have before you start college? What do you want to do before you get to college?

TEENS CAN DO GREAT THINGS!

Some people may think teenagers can't manage their time or do important things to affect the world, but that is simply not truth. You can do almost anything adults can do.

BUMBLE
BEES
CAN'T
FLY!

Here's an interesting scientific "fact": Did you know that **bumblebees can't fly!** It has been proven that it is impossible for a bumblebee to fly. If you simply look at the facts you would agree. Their bodies are too heavy and their wings are too light. They can't fly. However, bumblebees can't read scientific reports so they don't know they can't fly!

Why do you think they say bumblebees can't fly? Why do they? What do people say you can't do? Could it be you are like the bumblebee?

GREAT KIDS AND TEENS

Did you know that John Quincy Adams was the Russian ambassador to Catherine the Great when he was only fourteen years old? He performed musket drills with the Massachusetts Minute Men at age 8. At age 11, he was the official secretary to his father, John Adams, the Ambassador to the British. How did he do these great things at such a young age? It is obvious that his father saw his potential by making him the official secretary of an Ambassador.

In the 1700's David Faraguaet, joined the Navy when he was nine and took command of a captured British vessel when he was only twelve? Can you imagine a twelve year old commanding a big army warship today?

The hymn writer Francis Ridley Havergal could quote the whole New Testament and the book of Psalms by heart at the age of three. When she was five she could read the New Testament in the original Greek!

Mozart began composing music at the age of five. He performed for European royalty throughout his childhood and early teen years. Could you see yourself performing for the President?

My daughter, Anna, collected change and fed an entire orphanage for 2 years when she was only six years old. She had her first book published at 10. She began a Dance Team and choreographed her first ballet at 9.

These kids and teens are not special, they just used the gifts and talents they had to do great things. ALL teens and kids CAN do great things! I hope you will use these time management ideas long after this course is finished. Remember the famous words of Benjamin Franklin, "Failing to prepare is preparing to fail."

QUOTE OF THE DAY
"What you *get* by reaching your destination isn't nearly as important as what you *become* by reaching that destination."
Zig Ziglar

BREAK THE ELEPHANT CHAINS

Maybe you have a hard time believing that you could do great things. Often, we have heard things like "You can't do anything right" or "You'll never be good enough" or "You'll be just like your father." Those statements do not have to be true.

Have you ever noticed how they tie up elephants at the circus? An elephant is held by a small chain around his leg attached to a peg in the ground. It is very obvious that the chain could not stop the elephant, so what holds him there?

When the elephant was young, the same chain and peg could hold him. When it was first put on his leg, he pulled and tugged and could not get away. As he grew bigger, he didn't know the chain could not hold him any longer.

Just like the elephant, many of you are "chained" to the past. Words of discouragement you accepted as truth or things you couldn't do when you were younger still might hold you like that elephant. Don't let imaginary chains keep you from being all that you can be. Think about times you failed, someone made fun of you, or you were disappointed. You've grown since then! There is greatness inside each one of you just waiting to get out! Don't let those old "chains" keep you from being great!

JUMPING FLEAS

Capture some fleas and put them in a box with a lid. Watch what they do. The fleas will jump up and hit the lid a few times. Then, they will adjust their jumping height so as not to hit the top. After a while, take the lid off and watch them. Those silly fleas will STILL jump just high enough to avoid the lid, even after it is removed. Only a few brave ones will jump out of the jar.

Often, it is negative people or a past failures that convince you that you can't do anything great. They put a "lid" on your imagination and destroy your faith in your ability. Negative people will always be there. The key is to not to let those negative comments define who we are.

I learned a secret early in life I want to share with you. When we try something and it doesn't work, we haven't failed! We have simply learned what doesn't work.

You have greatness waiting to bust out of you. Do you have a LID keeping you from jumping out and being great in life? JUMP OUT OF YOUR BOX!

Henry Ford, the founder of the Ford Motor Company, wanted a V-8 engine designed. He had very little formal education. One day he thought up the idea of a V-8 engine. He called in his engineers and told them to build him a V-8. They explained all the reasons it could not be done. Ford didn't listen. He said, "Gentlemen, I must have a V-8 engine-build me one." They worked at it, but still did not produce one. They told him the V-8 was an absolute impossibility. He still did not listen. He said, "Gentlemen, you don't understand. I must have a V-8 engine and you are going to build it for me. Now go do it!" Guess what? The engineers figured it out and built the "impossible" V-8 Engine.

Get up and switch on the lights in your room. Thomas Edison invented the light bulb. Do you know how many "failures" it took to get it right? 900! But because he tried the 901th time, he isn't remembered for the 900 failures, but the one time that worked.

He stayed focused on his idea and continued to work on it until he got results. If there's something to do—don't let others or your own fears or past failures put a lid on you. Don't be limited by a short chain or a non-existent lid.

(Flea trainers, Elephants, Bumblebee and Henry Ford examples are adapted from Zig Ziglar motivational writings in "See You At the Top".)

WHAT CAN YOU DO?

How do you start doing big things like these children? Start small and keep climbing! You can make a difference in your community starting TODAY. Find somewhere to be nice today. Do a good deed in secret for someone.

Learn to take the INITIATIVE to do nice things for people. (INITIATIVE is doing something without being asked or prompted.)

Teens can do good things in their family and community. Sometimes, it is sneaking to make someone's bed before they get to it, or feeding the animals, or doing a chore around the house without being asked.

Sometimes, it is catching your neighbor gone and raking their yard or sweeping their porch secretly. It may be making lunches or gathering blankets to take to the homeless. It's fun to hide and watch as people find the good deeds.

Learn to take the INITIATIVE to go out of your way to do good things for people. It's the first step in becoming a life- changing person.

KEYS TO SUCCESS

Success is not dependent on who you are; what you look like; or how old, how tall, or what color you are. Successful people are simply ones who learn to use their unique talents, learn how to set goals and attain them, steward their time well, and do good to others.

Success is like a helium balloon. It's not what's on the outside—not it's shape, size, or color—that makes it rise. It's what's on the inside that makes it rise above everything else. The only limit to a balloon is the ceiling.

The only limit to your success is the ceiling of expectations from yourself and others as to what you can do. Remove the ceiling of can't do attitudes, negative thinking, and discouraging words out of your heart so that you can fly!

Take the ceiling off!
  YOU WILL FLY
    TO THE SKY!

  GREATNESS
is hidden inside you!

TAKE TIME TO BE SUCCESSFUL!

If you want to achieve great results—
You have to do it in a great way!

1. Never, NEVER say never!

2. Never, NEVER put other people down.

3. Never, NEVER put yourself down.

4. Always look for POTENTIAL and POSSIBILITY in yourself, in others, and in every challenge you face.

5. Use (invest) what you have NOW!

6. Don't take to heart others doubt, fear, unbelief, or words and attitudes about you or your dream. The only person who has to believe in it is YOU!

7. Don't take to heart words and attitudes that say young people can't do great things. Age has nothing to do with it!

8. Take TIME to do it right! Slow down and do the best job you can do. You deserve better than sloppy seconds.

9. Take TIME to imagine! The dreams and wishes living in your imagination are not silly! Imagination plays a big part in seeing dreams become reality! What you can SEE (in the window of your heart) you can ACHIEVE.

10. True success comes from taking the TIME to develop good character. Take time to build the right things inside.

11. Spend TIME with the right kind of people. Do you *really* want to act like, talk like, be like your friends, the person on TV, or character in a video game? *You become like who you hang out with.* With whom do you spend most of your time? Find someone to imitate who is inspiring and living life the right way.

12. Do everything you do with all the excellence you have right now—and keep growing better. You may not be able to draw like a professional artist today but do your art the very best that you can for your age and someday you will.

13. Climb on the shoulders of a great person who inspired you and take it higher. Read everything you can about your most inspiring person, meet them and talk with them if possible. Study their success and what makes them a success. Don't

be satisfied with just their level of success but realize that each generation does it a little better.

14. Be a good LIFE manager. You don't have to wait until you're through college to use your life skills of success.

15. Don't think SMALL! No one judges an adult's ability by how tall or short he is—unless it is for playing on a professional basketball team. Dynamite comes in small packages!

16. Take time to PLAY. Don't look down on things you do that are fun!

17. Take TIME to recharge your energy cells. You need down time to contemplate life and rest when you don't have to do anything to truly be a success.

18. Keep your PRIORITIES right throughout life. Keep family, health, others feelings, your faith, and whatever is important to you before success. I often encourage parents to not work so hard FOR their family that they FORGET their family.

QUIZ 9
INITIATIVE

1. What is initiative?

2. Who was an ambassador at age 14?

3. Why do elephants not run away when pinned by a tiny stake in the ground?

4. Why is greatness not dependent on size, color, and shape of the person?

XIII.
FAMILY TIME

QUOTE OF THE DAY
"Think naught a trifle,
though it small appear:
Small sands the
mountain, moments
make the year, And
trifles life."
Edward Young

XIII. FAMILY TIME

Parents have so many responsibilities! They are busy with work, household chores, cooking, shopping, paying bills and many other responsibilities necessary to run the household. Do you ever feel your parents don't have enough time to spend with you?

__Yes ___ No ___ Sometimes

What are some things that keep your parents busy? Check the things that your parents seem to be always doing:

__ WORKING
__ HOUSEHOLD CHORES
__ TALKING ON THE PHONE OR TEXTING
__ EMAILING OR INTERNET
__ WATCHING TV
__ BUSINESS MEETINGS
__ CHURCH ACTIVITIES
__ DRIVING YOU AND YOUR BROTHERS AND SISTERS TO ACTIVITIES

Do you have family time to talk about things each day? Talk to your parents today about how important they are in your life. Value their input! Make an "appointment" with each of your parents to do something special this week, just the two of you.

A FAMILY IDEA

Who does the chores at your home? Often most of that responsibility falls on your mother. Mothers seem to have a talent at asking kids to take out the trash or do the dishes just as a favorite program comes on or right in the middle of an important level on a video game. Your response might be, "Can I do it as soon as this program goes off?" Problem is, by the time you finish the program you often forget to do what was asked. By the time your mom asks you three or four times to take out the trash, she gets frustrated because it would have been easier to do it herself.

As a mom, I found a great solution. It kept me from asking over and over and kept my son from getting upset when I was constantly interrupting his video game at a critical moment. We found out, too, that if we shared the load there was time to go to the soccer field to practice with him every afternoon. Here's the idea that changed our chores each day to a stress free task. It's easy to remember and fair for everyone.

Put an erasable board on the refrigerator. Each day have your parents jot down all the little jobs that need to be done for that day. Each child (and parent) must pick two jobs to do each day.

(Younger ones may only do one job and have * for ones that they can handle.) Obviously, the earlier you do your chores, the easier jobs are available to be chosen. This eliminates one person taking on all the responsibility of running the household and leaves quality family time for everyone everyday! This process also clearly defines when work is "done" since there seems to always be something else that can be done around the house!

Put a magnetic grocery list pad on the refrigerator and each time someone uses the last of something in the household, write it on the list. At shopping time the shopping list is ready and your Mom never forgets to get your shampoo or favorite cereal!

Another idea is to use the TEAMWORK chart on the next page. Assign tasks to each person for the week, and work as a team to get the job done. Be sure to mix up the jobs so everyone gets a chance at trying everything!

Finally, when all the chores are finished, have some family fun! Go to the park, play a game together, or go get an ice cream cone. Spend some time together as a family each and every day. Often teens, as they are trying to establish their own identity, forget the value of their family. As teens mature into young adults, they realize family is a treasure.

WHAT WOULD YOU LIKE TO DO?

Talk about fun activities you would like to do sometime such as a picnic, bowling, putt-putt, swimming, going on a hike, or other special outing. Ask if there are ways you can help around the house to give your parents more time to do fun things.

THINGS I WOULD LIKE TO DO

_____

_____

_____

_____

_____

_____

_____

What do you and your friends do together? How does spending time with someone help the relationship to grow?

How do you think spending fun time with your family might affect your household?

TEAMWORK TASKS

NAME_____	S	M	T	W	R	F	S
_____							
_____							
_____							
_____							
_____							

NAME_____	S	M	T	W	R	F	S
_____							
_____							
_____							
_____							
_____							

NAME_____	S	M	T	W	R	F	S
_____							
_____							
_____							
_____							
_____							

NAME_____	S	M	T	W	R	F	S
_____							
_____							
_____							
_____							
_____							

NAME_____	S	M	T	W	R	F	S
_____							
_____							
_____							
_____							
_____							

GREAT TEAMWORK!!

FAMILY MEETINGS

One way to maintain a good family relationship is regular and open communication. Communication is more that saying hello or discussing what's for dinner. Communication involves your feelings, and what is important to you. Learn to talk about things that matter to your parents.

We usually have discussions only when problems arise or leave little issues unsettled until they blow up. If issues were handled on a week to week basis they would rarely escalate into the monster issues that cause division and pain in relationships.

Ask your parents to consider a family meeting each week. Have a set time to meet. Parents, for a successful family meeting, don't use the time to lecture and correct. See it as a time to build your family and get input from everyone. A hand needs input from all the fingers to work properly. In the same way, all members of the family have ideas and solutions that can make the family work better as a team.

When you go away to college, these meetings can be a way to stay connected to your family as well. At that time, they will become more important to you.

FAMILY MEETING IDEAS

Try to accomplish these objectives:

1. Each member needs to bring their schedules, commitments, outings they would like to attend, and other schedule items to fit into the family calendar.

2. Each person should jot down little issues or ideas they would like to present to the family throughout the week. If it concerns one person, have a break out session time where you can discuss one on one if needed. Otherwise, talk through issues as a family and set up a plan of action on how you are going to handle it.

3. Brings goals and objectives for the month or year together and discuss them together. Give each other time to think over them and make an appointment to get back together to see how each one feels about it.

4. Bring something to celebrate from your life this week. Take time to share with the family in this time of fellowship and unity.

Some guidelines for parents:

- KEEP IT SHORT!
 Children have a short attention span.

- TAKE TIME to listen to the little members of the family.

If you take what children or younger brothers and sisters have to say of importance in the meeting, they will contribute more and more. Sometimes you need a 4-year-old's perspective of life. They may want to celebrate that lightning bugs came out or to pray for a sick goldfish. Young children help adults see the beautiful things in life which we often miss with our busy lives!

TAKE TIME TO APPRECIATE YOUR FAMILY

If you ever feel like you wish you didn't have to put up with your little brother or big sister, or didn't have to listen to your parents, do this test: Take five minutes and imagine your life without them. What if they were gone tomorrow? This little exercise helps us appreciate each and every member.

FAMILY MEETING AGENDA

Meeting time and date:_____

1. Things I want to add to the family TIME calendar:

Appointments_____

Meetings or Events_____

Outings_____

Things I would LIKE to do_____

2. My Ideas and Issues in my life:

_____
_____
_____

3. Goals and Things to Do:_____

_____
_____
_____

4. Treasures- Something good that happened this week to share with the family

_____
_____

FUN FACTS

The first encounter you or your family has in the morning affects the rest of their day more than the next 5 put together!

Start your day right! Be kind and agreeable in the morning to your family, and to your friends when you get to school. It will make your entire day better!

Do you want to make another person feel as if they are important to you? When you are talking to them, take the time to stop and look at them and think to yourself, "This is the most important person in the whole world." Your body language and attention will communicate that thought without saying a word. VALUE your friends and family!

 This is the most important person in the world!

The intimacy level established in the first four minutes when someone returns home sets the stage for all evening. Take 4 minutes to celebrate your family returning! It'll make the entire evening run smoother and everyone feel closer.

A Family is a
T.E.A.M.-
Together
Everyone
Accomplishes
More

XIV.
PROCRASTINATION

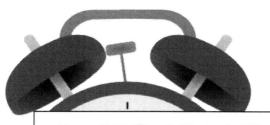

QUOTE OF THE DAY
"Never put off til'
tomorrow
what you can do today."
Author Unknown

XIII. PROCRASTINATION

Procrastination is my sin.
It brings me constant sorrow.
I really must do something about it.
Perhaps I'll start tomorrow.

Pro-cras-ti-nate means to put things off. It starts out innocently usually. You know you need to do something, but decide to put it off until tomorrow or next week. That is called PROCRASTINATION! You usually find that the next day comes and you are either busy or totally forget what you intended to do.

Sometimes procrastination comes from not knowing where to start or how to do the job. Other times it is a fear of failure so you just don't start. Other times it is simply laziness or lack of priorities. Whatever the reason, the solution is to learn to overcome procrastination.

Let's begin this chapter on procrastination by evaluating where your time is going again. I know we have done this exercise several times this year, but your time requirements and use of time is constantly changing.

TOTAL 24 hours:

Sleep _____

School _____

Chores _____

Quiet Time _____

Church _____

Creative Time _____

Exercise _____

Family time _____

Friends _____

TV/games/internet_____

How full is your time? Where do you spend most of your time?

Add up all your TV, video, computer time and compare it to exercise. Add up all your "friend" time and compare it to time with family. How well are you "stewarding" your time?
("Steward" means to use what you have the best way possible.)

"What I do today is important because I am paying a day of my life for it."
Author Unknown

QUOTE OF THE DAY
"Success is not a destination, it's a journey, it's the direction in which you are traveling."
Oliver Wendall Holmes

Four Kinds of Procrastination:

A. Attitudinal Procrastination
This kind of procrastination may be rooted in fear of failure, unwilling to tolerate unpleasantness, fear of success, low self-esteem, depression, shyness

B. Cognitive Procrastination
Cognitive Procrastination may be the cause because of unclear priorities, indecisiveness, inadequate information

C. Environmental Procrastination
Clutter, disorganization, noise, unmanageable workloads can all stagnate your productivity through environmental procrastination.

D. Physiological Procrastination
Body weakness such as fatigue, stress, or illness can produce physiological procrastination.

One key to overcoming procrastination is to determine why you have the problem. Looking at the list above, why do YOU procrastinate?

Other Vices to your TIME that Can Cause Procrastination:

1. Floundering - Failure to focus in one direction

2. Wheel Spinning - Busy but not productive

3. Fire Fighting - Schedule time around opportunities, not problems

4. Vacillating - Indecisiveness

5. Dawdling - Work expands to fit time available

6. Spraying – Going in too many directions

7. Switching - Partly finished projects

8. Acquiescing – Not able to say NO enough

9. Rehashing – Dwelling in past

10. Perfecting - strive for excellence, not perfection to the point it paralyzes

STOP PROCRASTINATING WITH HOMEWORK

To break the habit of procrastination for homework, try these ideas to help.

- Lay out a time to do each assignment and when you are going to do it.

- Break big projects into steps and do one step a day.

- Plan time to start it and time to get it done.

- Salami technique- list all the steps to get it done and do one at a day

- 15 minute plan- set a timer and force yourself to spend 15 minutes daily on your task

- Do the worst part first. Then you will not procrastinate because you dread that part.

- Balance sheet or The Ben Franklin Approach- list all the reasons for not doing it on one side, all the benefits to doing it on the other

PROCRASTINATION BUSTING!

Make a list of all the things you have been putting off. It could be cleaning out your closet, doing a big assignment, or cleaning your room. Take ONE item and go through the procrastination busting procedures this week, one at a time. We are going to use the example of cleaning your room in this example.

DAY 1: Use the Ben Franklin approach

List all the reasons on the left for not doing the job including any consequences to not doing it. List all the benefits for doing it on the right.

NOT DO
    Takes too much time
    Favorite TV Program on
    Don't like to do it

TO DO
can't find soccer ball
need clean jeans
can't have friends in
Won't get allowance
Lost my earring

DAY 2: Salami Approach

Make a detailed list of all the steps to complete the job. If you made a routine for cleaning your room print out that page. For ones who procrastinated, now you have to do it!☺

Cleaning Steps
1. Make my bed (or change the sheets)
2. Put dirty clothes in laundry room
3. Put away clean laundry from basket
4. Put books on shelf or closet (remember to organize or sort into like things to find them later)
5. Put library books in "Out" Box by front door
6. Empty any cans and throw in recycle
7. Straighten up shelves
8. Empty trash can
9. Vacumn

Now do one or two steps today…and every day this week. By Friday your room will be all clean and start over on Monday! TA-DA— a clean room that stays clean if you do one little step a day once it is clean!

DAY 3: Do the Worst First

Do the part of your list that you dread doing first today and get it over with. Then you will have that out of the way and won't have to do it again!

Which part of cleaning your room do you dislike the most? Do it first—then you don't have to dread it. Exception, don't take the trash until you've gathered the trash. Don't take clothes to the laundry until you've picked them all up. You've got the idea, don't make double work for yourself!

DAY 4: Try the 15 minute approach

Set an alarm clock and work on your room for 15 minutes in the morning. Stop when you hear the alarm. Do the same thing in the afternoon.

Take your list from above and work 15 minutes on anything or all of it. Stop when the alarm sounds every day.

DAY 5: See how many steps you have left to do.

"Guesstimate" (take an educated guess) as to how much time each step will take and jot it beside the step. Take your "cleaning room" list and estimate the time to do each job. Divide it by 5 and do that many minutes each day.

If it is an assignment, how many days do you have left before it is due? Divide the total time to complete the project by the number of days left. Work that many minutes today on your project.

DAY 6: Stick with the plan

Use either the Salami approach, the 15 minute approach, or the Guesstimate approach today and every day until the task is completed

Helpful Hint

I always plan MORE time than I think I need in case I have misjudged time necessary or in case problems arise. PLAN to be finished at least one day before you need to be.

QUOTE OF THE DAY
"If you have any duty
which must be done,
and it seems disagreeable,
do it promptly
and have it over."
Thomas Jefferson

QUIZ 10
FAMILY/PROCRASTINATION

1. The first____ minutes when someone returns home establishes the intimacy level all evening.

2. The first encounter of the morning has more effect than the next ___ put together.

3. What does T.E.A.M. mean?

4. Procrastination is the _____ of time.

5. What does procrastination mean?

6. List three ways to overcome procrastination:

XV. TIME SUCCESS HOT POINTS REVIEW

QUOTE OF THE DAY
"Destiny is not
a matter of chance,
it is a matter of choice;
it is not a thing to be waited for,
it is a thing to be achieved."
William Jennings Bryant

XIV. TIME SUCCESS HOT POINTS REVIEW

- ## TIME LOGS FOR WEEK

  We need structure. The human body was designed to function in structure. Your brain needs a pattern to follow. Don't fall into bad time habits. Don't vary get up time or eating times. Otherwise, you will feel irritable and sluggish and cannot accomplish as much. Get a good routine and give it 3 weeks to settle. It takes 21 days to form a habit.

  Keep a TIME LOG again. Compare your time usage to the first one you did earlier in the year. See how your time management has changed.

- ## TAKE TIME TO PLAN

  MAKE time to plan out your week and review assignments due and progress. WRITE DOWN Goals/To Do Lists! It is vital in effective time management. A TO DO List is a commitment to YOU. Remember the Saccadic Eye Motion experiment? Your brain still NEEDS a pattern to follow every day.

- ## WRITE IT DOWN
  You are 30% more likely to accomplish it by writing it down. (You have a model "stuff to do" sheet on the next page.) Make copies and plan your week! Be sure to PLAN a time for friends, time to spend time with family, and free time for yourself.

- ## LACK OF FOCUS
  People spend 1/3 of their waking hours in daydreams. What's on my mind? Is it robbing me of 1/3 of my day? Make little notes that say, "WHAT'S ON MY MIND NOW?" Tape them up everywhere you will see them in a day. Put one on the mirror, on your desk, by your bed, in your notebook, and in the car. Every time you see those notes, take a minute to write down what you are thinking. Is it positive? Are you thinking about what you should be or is your mind wandering? (ie: in school is your mind wandering from the teacher?)

  Is it a healthy, positive thought? Does it put you or someone else down or edify? Now, change what you are thinking and get back on track. Use these little signs to check your thoughts. When you see them, pull your thoughts back into productive ones and remove any negative thinking about yourself and others.

STUFF TO DO!!!

NAME_____	S	M	T	W	R	F	S

NAME_____	S	M	T	W	R	F	S

NAME_____	S	M	T	W	R	F	S

NAME_____	S	M	T	W	R	F	S

NAME_____	S	M	T	W	R	F	S

• WATCH WHAT YOU SAY

Hide a tape recorder and listen to what you say about yourself, about school, about life. Is it a "I'll never be able to do this" attitude? Did you know your words are like the rudder of a ship? They control the direction of your life.

If you SAY "I can't do anything", you will be more likely to not be able to do it. Your expectation plays a big role in what you can and can't accomplish in life. Decide today to rid your mouth of negative, failure type words. Instead, develop an "I CAN" attitude and vocabulary. If you apply yourself, the day will come when you can do anything you think you can do!

Take a few minutes today to write down all the good qualities about yourself. Begin to read that list out loud to yourself every day for a week. You will be surprised at how it changes the way you see yourself!

• TAKE THE INITIATIVE

Take the initiative to do more than is expected of you in school, in your family life, and in the community. Do you remember what initiative means? It is to do something without being asked. Look for opportunities to go above and beyond expectations. That kind of attitude will cause you to succeed in every area of life.

When I was in high school, I had a special teacher for Math 5 and Computer Programming. His name was Charlie Joe Allen. Mr. Allen was a great Math teacher. He was an even greater life teacher.

I was usually almost a straight A student. Imagine my surprise the first time I turned in a "perfect" computer program to find my grade was only a "B". I stayed after class to ask what I had done wrong. He assured me I had written a program exactly the way he assigned it. "So why didn't I get an A?" I insisted.

His answer has changed the course of my life. He said, "I never give an A on a program unless you go above and beyond what I assign. "

From that point on, I got A's on my programs. I also I learned to TAKE THE INTIATIVE in life. It has been life changing.

Surprise your parents today!
Do more than they ask of you. If they ask you to empty the trash in your room, do it for the entire house.

Surprise your teacher!
Do a few extra problems for extra credit. Get to class early and ask if you can help in any way.

- ## DON'T MULTI-TASK STUDY

A recent study of the National Academy of Science found that your parents were right....sorry.☺ Watching TV or listening to distracting music while studying blocks your brain from remembering information long term. This is the tricky part, distractions do not seem to make a big difference in short term memory. If you choose to study with distractions, by the end of the semester you will not remember what you studied. That means MORE study time! If you don't want to spend time re-learning for semester tests— turn off the distractions and you will remember much more!

- ## MAKE A FILING SYSTEM

For School work— make a "TO DO", "TO READ", and "TO FILE" folder and carry your folders with you or a book to read. When you have to wait for a few minutes, read a chapter of a book, write a letter, or plan your next day. Carry something that can be done in a few minutes and doesn't require a lot of concentration. USE waiting time. There are little pieces of time all day that can be used rather than wasted if you have something with you that you need to do.

- **MAKE NOTE TAKING A HABIT** both in class and when reading. It is much easier to review your notes for finals than to try to review the entire textbook. A LITTLE extra time in daily study will make final week much easier! A different part of your brain is used when you write it down so you are more likely to remember it.

- **ESTABLISH ROUTINES**

  Do the same thing every performance. Have you ever noticed that ten minutes before the end of the circus you'll see clowns still running around, trapeze artists still on the ropes, and the animal trainer still in center ring with a tiger. But as the 5:00 ending time draws near, suddenly everything is finished and in its place. The circus ends right on time. Why is that? They do the same thing every performance.

  Your day will be much smoother if you stick with a routine. Work out a homework routine and put it on paper. Then, when your mom tells you to do your homework, go to your routine and do it with excellence every time.

- # DON'T OVERLOAD!

  With sports, school and homework, friends and social events, dance/gymnastic/piano/guitar/or other music lessons, scouts, church youth group, part time jobs, and family requirements; it is easy to overload your schedule. If you overload it is hard to do anything really well. Are you spread too thin?

  Find out what is expected of you around the household and with the family. Pick one or two outside activities that are very important to you and concentrate on them. It is better to become really good at one or two things than to be spread so thin you never feel a sense of accomplishment.

  Be sure to include your parents in your scheduling. They have their own schedules and the schedules of other siblings to work into household time needs.

- # REWARD YOURSELF

  When you finish the things you want to do, treat yourself to something you like to do or eat. Celebrate yourself even if no one else does! Humans respond to rewards, even if you reward yourself!

- ## AVOID LAST MINUTE STRESS

  If you have soccer starting this weekend; plan time at the first of the week to check shoes, socks, and shin guards for fit in advance. You may need to buy or repair something. If you have a term paper due Friday, be certain you have scheduled time to type it or buy special folders needed to finish the job. Avoid last minute panic! If you are planning to clean out the garage, be sure to have adequate boxes and cleaning supplies to get the job done without running to the store to get something to finish it up. Planning ahead makes life run smoother!

- ## FINISH BEFORE MOVING ON

  It is easier to stick with homework, clean out your closet, or do other big tasks. Finish the job rather than spreading it out. Each time you stop requires time to get refocused.

- ## PLAN BEFORE YOU START

  Before starting assignments be certain you have everything you'll need to complete the tasks. Plan what to wear the night before and lay out your clothes to make a smoother morning.

• HANDLE THINGS ONCE

If you throw your coat, backpack, and shoes in a corner when you come in, later you have to go back and put them where they belong.   Put a shoe basket and coat hanger by your bedroom door. When you leave, everything is right there! When you finish homework, pack your backpack for the next day and sit it by your coat. You'll never forget a book or assignment again! If you have any books or movies to return, put them in an "out the door" box by the front door. Then, your mom will never forget the things that need to go out as she does errands.

GREATNESS RISES
Helium Balloons go up because of what's on the INSIDE of them, not what's on the outside.
It doesn't matter what shape, size, or color the balloon. You won't be great because of something on the outside of you, Greatness is found on the inside!

QUIZ 11
TIME TIPS

1. Why do we need time lists?

2. People spend _____ of their day in daydreams on average.

3. Watching TV or listening to distracting music while studying blocks your _____ memory.

4. Why should we have a routine to follow?

5. Why should you reward yourself when you complete a task?

6. List some ways to avoid last minute stress.

Have You Tried It?

In the family chapter, you learned that the first encounter you or your family has in the morning affects the rest of their day more than the next 5 put together!

Have you made an effort to begin your day right? Has it made a difference?

We also discussed that the intimacy level established in the first four minutes when someone returns home sets the stage for all evening.

Have you added these very important four minutes to your day?

XVI.
TIME THIEVES

"Do not allow
idleness to deceive
you;
for while you give
him today,
he steals tomorrow
from you."
A. F. Forester

XVI. EXTERNAL TIME THIEVES

There are two kinds of time thieves in your life. There are "external" ones that attack your time from the outside. There are also internal ones. These are attitudes and limitations that come from inside you. External thieves are easier to change than internal. Let's look at common external time thieves first.

TV-VIDEO GAMES-MOVIES-INTERNET-TEXTS

These habits can steal your life away if you let them! The average high school graduate spends about 2-3 hours watching television daily (16-18 hours weekly), and average internet users stay on the computer 3 hours per day (21 hours weekly). Factor in video games and movies too and you spend 35-55 hours in front of a screen EVERY WEEK. You may be spending 15 hours a week more than a normal 40-hour workweek on a TIME THIEF!

American teens (13-19) sent an average of 2,272 texts per month in 2008. That's 80 texts daily.**

An 18 year old has watched over 18,000 hours of television by the time they graduate high school. That's over 5000 more hours than they spent on their 12 years of classes! American kids spend more time on TV than any other activity except sleeping. Why sit and watch others be what they dreamed in life when you can INVEST that time in turning your life into something people watch????

*Statistics from www.clickz.com/stats/sectors/demographics
**Statistics from Neilson Company 2009

- ## SOCIAL DISTRACTIONS!
  BE CAREFUL- Don't let your social life steal your success. Don't let friends draw you from your greatness! Plan study time when your household is not distracting. It is difficult to study when your younger brother has friends over playing. Be WISE in this area!

- ## DON'T GET OVER LOADED
  Intermural Sports/Clubs/Music Ensembles are all good things but don't join everything on campus! Pick one or two and get involved. Find out what time commitments are required. Keep the priority of your purpose to get an education to train for life.

- ## AVOID NEGATIVE PEOPLE
  Don't spend a large amount of your free time with negative people. They will pull you down. You reflect (begin to look like) the company you

keep. Surround yourself with high achievers in school, sports, friends who have healthy, loving relationships with family.

I heard a story one time, that helps us see why it is important to not listen to people who look at everything from a critical or negative perspective.

A woman looked out her window and watched the neighbor hanging her clothes out to dry. She criticized every day about how dingy the clothes looked. She could not understand why the woman did not clean her laundry for her family.

One morning she got up and looked out her window. The neighbor was hanging out laundry again, but they were sparkling white! She was so excited that she called her husband to see. "Look, Honey, she finally got their laundry clean." Her husband said, "Actually, I got up early and cleaned our windows."

You see, it was the window she was looking through that was the problem, not the neighbor's laundry.

Your ears are not garbage cans. Don't listen to their negative poison about you or anyone else!

- **AVOID BAD COUNSEL**
  Being pulled into wrong directions wastes TIME. Friends are not always right. Check their life before you follow their path! Don't give in to peer pressure. Learn to seek wise counsel. Ask your youth leader, parents, teacher, or a school counselor's input for problems.

- **ELIMINATE DISORGANIZATION**
  Make a place for everything in your room and put it back! Set a basket by the door for your backpack, keys, purse, videos and library books to return, etc. When there is something you are going to need the next day, put in the OUT THE DOOR basket. You'll never forget things!

- **DON'T WASTE TIME FORGETTING**
  Put a magnetic shopping list pad on your refrigerator. When you are running low on something or think of something you need from the store—jot it down. When you mom is ready to shop you don't waste time seeing what you need, or worse yet, go to the store without a list. Inevitably, you will forget something and have to make another trip!

• CONTROL INTERRUPTIONS

The most common threat to your day is the problem of interruptions. Concentration requires dedication and no interruptions. Jot down every interruption for the next two or three days, both unexpected telephone calls and texts as well as interruptions in person. Keep a log of who it was, what was the reason for the interruption, and how long it took to resume your homework or whatever you were doing.

Teenagers have the biggest challenge in this area. Texts and phone calls are a minute by minute problem. The average teen texts 80 times each day. Having close friends is not the problem, however learning to manage your time around friends to avoid constant interruptions is a must for teens today. Each interruption breaks your train of concentration. Each time you stop to check a text or grab a call, it takes several minutes to get back to the same concentration level. It adds minutes or perhaps hours to your weekly homework time.

My suggestion is this: block off time for the homework and put your phone in a place you are not tempted to check your texts when they come in. After finishing homework, or if you can't wait that long take a break after you finish each assignment. Return all your texts and calls in that 15 minute break. Leave the phone again, and get back to work. It will shave hours off your homework time each week to have MORE time to do things with your friends!

Telephones are an essential part of life but we must learn to control their interruptive nature. Though most people resist this one, it is more efficient to have messages collect and return all your calls at a designated time in your schedule.

If a friend calls who needs to talk at length and it is not a convenient time, find out when would be a good time to return the call. Many of my family's calls are from my husband's students. I have learned to screen the calls by seeing if I can help them rather than constantly interrupting him to take the call.

If someone is especially demanding I will often ask, "Ben is busy now, would you like for me to interrupt him?" People do not like to feel they are an interruption unless it is really important.

INTERRUPTIONS will be your main external thief for the rest of your life. Learn how to manage it now!

INTERNAL TIME THIEVES

PROCRASTINATION is one of the main internal time thieves. We've already talked about it, but let's review strategies to overcome it again!

1. Determine starting and planned completion time

2. Salami technique: list steps and do one at a time

3. 15 minute plan: set a timer and force yourself to spend 15 minutes daily

4. Do the worst part first. Then you will not procrastinate because you hate it!

5. Balance sheet: (Ben Franklin) list all the reasons for procrastination on one side, all the benefits to do it on the other

> Procrastination is NOT
> a weakness
> you are stuck with
> but instead a habit that
> CAN be changed.

STRESS

Another internal time thief is stress. Stress prevents us from functioning at maximum potential. Teenagers are feeling the pressures of life and can be stressed, too.

If you have stomach problems, trouble sleeping or restless sleep, find yourself accident prone, heart palpitations, or getting sick and having headaches more than others, it may be caused by stress. It may be your body sending you signals to slow down.

There are three stages of stress.

#1- Alarm- this is the fight stage of stress. It is when the adrenaline pumps for the height to meet the challenges. It produces a chemical depression afterwards and can cause ulcers and heart disorders. Each new stressor or stressful situation damages the body.

#2- Resistance- At this stage we begin to try to deal with the stress. We attempt to adjust the pressure and handle emotions such as anxiety when it shows up. Depression, low frustration level and tolerance are signs of this stage. The immune system breaks down and we become more susceptible to disease.

#3- Exhaustion- Physical and psychological exhaustion sets in over a period of time. We are unable to maintain a sense of personal equilibrium and become dysfunctional during this stage. The last stage of exhaustion is death.

Symptoms of stress include a disrupted thought process. This is a major cause of accidents. Body tissue is broken down from stress. Each stressful encounter leaves a chemical scar that, over time, deteriorates more rapidly. Signs that tissue breakdown is occurring are fatigue, headaches, back pain, extreme tiredness, vulnerability to illness, muscular tension, no energy, and insomnia.

According to the Centers for Disease Control, over 1/4 of high schoolers have seriously considered suicide at some point.

If you are feeling stress from being overloaded, complicated situations at home, trying to perform on a sports or dance team, or from others expectations; here are a few ideas to help you be less stressed:

- Reset your inner clock and watch things that make you feel stressed. Discuss stressful things in your life with your parents.

- Get adequate sleep. Get up the same time each day. Dramatic changes in weekend/weekday get up times produces fatigue.

- If you feel pressure from big assignments and can't sleep because you are thinking about it, write down all you need to do on a piece of paper before you go to bed. It will free your mind of the problem. The next day, pick it back up.

- Don't spend time worrying! Negative emotions, worry, offense, and fear literally send a toxic chemical into your body. Fear can cause your memory "trees" to choke off and block accessing information for tests.

  - Lower expectations of yourself. Be realistic!

  - Talk through problems. Get support.

  - Practice good breathing. Deep breaths release a chemical in your bloodstream to reduce stress.

  - Have a good cry. Tears release a chemical that calms.

  - Don't forget to give and get hugs!

- Take time to PLAY. Successful people learn the art of just being able to have fun.

- Find ways to express your creativity. Science projects, music, dance, or drama are all sources to use your creativity. When you are excited about something you truly enjoy, it makes life more fun and relaxing

- Have a good LAUGH. A hearty laugh can relieve stress, boost your immune system, and help you relax. It has been said that 20 seconds of laughing has the equivalent effect on the body of a 90 second sprint.

QUIZ 12
TIME THIEVES

1. There are _____ and _____ time thieves.

2. The average 18 year old has spent _____ watching TV in his life.

3. You _____ the company you keep.

4. Who is a good person to ask for counsel?

5. Name two external time thieves.

6. Name two internal time thieves.

7. What are some ways to overcome stress?

OTHER TIPS
TO MANAGE YOUR DAY

- **Get started**! Quit procrastinating!

- **Raise your energy level** by lowering the temperature

- **Stay on task.** Don't jump from one thing to another. You will feel like you never do anything if you never finish anything.

- **Do what you don't like first**! Get the worst part out of the way!

- **Emphasis WHAT you do and not how long you work**- focus on PRODUCTIVITY not ACTIVITY.

- **DO it right the 1st time**- it takes time to re-do!

- **Utilize each other's strengths.** You each have things you can do well and efficiently. Your friends and family have strengths that may be different. Learn to maximize your TEAM by recognizing strengths.

- **Accountability-** We all need to be held accountable for our time! Let others see your "things I am procrastinating about" page and ask them to hold you accountable and check up on your progress in a non-condemning way.

- **Flexible schedule-** PLAN to have some flexibility in your life. Don't "over plan" your life so that it becomes rigid.

- **Avoid perfectionism-** Don't expect a younger brother or sister to perform a job as well as you do-. You've had lots of practice. Don't be too hard on yourself, either. It takes time to develop skills.

- **Trust your abilities-** You can do more than you think you can! Remember about the elephant chains and flea trainers!

- **Use a PROCESS-** A circus is precise because it does the same thing every time. Develop a process for things and you will be more efficient.

- **Handle papers once-** Don't just shift things around to another location. Use the TO DO- TO READ-TO FILE and the TRASH CAN system.

- **Keep a master TO DO List**- don't clutter your daily list with all the long term projects. Take items off your long term project list and put on daily list as you can accomplish them.

- **Use the little blocks of "five minutes"** here and there all day. Note the little time things on your to do list and make one call, do one job, read one story. Don't discount the value of 5 minutes!

- **USE waiting time**- waiting to be picked up, waiting in line, waiting for others to get ready….USE the time instead of throwing it away. Make a list of things you can do in 5 minutes, in 15 minutes, and in 30 minutes.

- **LAUGH!!!!** Enjoy life, when things get overloaded, just laugh

- **Be sure to include time to just have nothing to do.** Creativity is birthed in those moments.

- **Plan time to talk** with your parents about your day. Bedtime is a good time to discuss anything bothering you or problems you are facing.

- Get an I CAN do this attitude! Success is 90% belief.

XVII.
TIME FOR
COLLEGE
PREPARATION

QUOTE OF THE DAY
"By failing to prepare,
you are
preparing to fail."
Benjamin Franklin

XVII. COLLEGE PLANNING

College is a unique experience. Many of you will be on your own for the first time. You'll be managing not only school but managing life on your own. You will move into a world without your parents to do things you have not even had to think about the past eighteen years. You'll make mistakes, and learn from them.

An area you need to be considering now is what you want to do with your life. Often I speak with college students who change majors several times because they did not go into college with a clear picture of what they wanted to do. That often means taking classes for one major you don't even need for another major—wasting time and money. If you are unsure of your major when enrolling in college, take ONLY core curriculum needed by any major the first semester while you are still seeking direction.

Be sure to check out classes in the spring BEFORE you enroll for fall semester. Talk to students to see what teachers are the best and which courses are hardest or easiest. As you PLAN your schedule around your natural body strengths, plan those tough classes during your peak times. Also, plan independent study time in those same peak times if you don't have classes scheduled there each day.

One big potential for failure in college is not knowing how to manage your time with the freedom college allows. Too often, social life derails the academic life with the freedom of choice of time. That often leads to drop outs and failure in college, especially for freshmen.

You really can have time for classes, homework, extra curricular, and still have time for fun with your friends. Time demands simply have to be prioritized. Taking this course in high school will help instill habits that will make the transition to college much easier.

The first major difference you will find in college is the shift from classroom time to independent study or homework time. In high school, you were in class 7 hours with one or two of homework daily. (40-45 hours weekly)

You need to plan AT LEAST that much time each week into your schedule for class/homework in college, even though time in class will be reduced, the workload will increase. Plan 3 hours daily for homework.

High School Minimum Time Required = 45 hours per week (7x5=35 Hours of Classes weekly + 2x5= 10 Hours of Homework weekly)

A good way to consider your time in college is to "be in school mode" the same hours you were in high school. If you are talking 16 hours of classes, plan about twice that much time for outside work for those classes. Plan 3-5 hours daily to work out side of class each day, depending on what subjects you are taking this semester.

The second thing about college classes that can derail your time is that classes are not always consecutive. Usually, classes are spread out through the day with breaks in between. Some students I've taught in work shops have used the in between class time to do homework at the library. This keeps their focus on academics to keep their minds on school all day. Plus, it is a quiet place to study and focus without distractions.

That much homework may seem impossible, but it is not really much more time consuming than high school. You simply have to manage your time and keep your focus on school and things to succeed in school first before socializing. You have 24 hours in a day- 8 for sleeping leaves 16 hours for everything else!   There IS time for class, homework, and social!

For 12 credit hours

2.4 hours class daily + 2.4-5 hours study daily=4.4-7.4 hours daily for school. Which leaves 9-12 hours discretionary time daily +weekends to catch up or free time if you apply yourself during the week

For 16 credit hours

3.2 hours class daily+4-6.4 hours study daily=6-9 hours daily school, which leaves 5-8 hours of discretionary time daily + weekends.

If you are in sports that may require 4-6 hours daily for practice and games, which only leaves 2-4 hours a day + weekends for everything else.

It REALLY isn't that much more school time than high school. It is simply shifting the responsibility of learning the material to being your own responsibility.

 12 hours of class + 24 hours of outside class study = 36 hours per week for school

16 hours of class + 32 hours of outside class study = 48 hours per week for school
(which is about the same time requirement as high school! You CAN do it!)

Time COUNTS! Swap just 30 minutes per day from Television to Studying, practicing, training, or your dreams for after college and in one year you will have invested 182.5 hours or 22.8 - 8 hour working days in 1 year!!!!! How many years have you had a dream in your heart? How would 30 minutes daily have added up? Multiply it out!

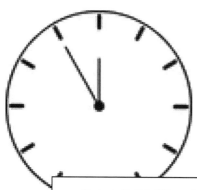

QUOTE OF THE DAY
Let us not
go over the old ground
but rather prepare
for what is to come.
Cicero

COLLEGE GOALS

Many times students go into college without goals for their time. That is a huge mistake. Take some time this week to consider what you would like to accomplish in college.

Your teachers will have a goal for you: a course of study for you to master. Your coaches will have a goal for your team and you if you play sports in college: to win the games. Your parents will have a goal for you: to finish college. Your girlfriend may have a goal for you: to get married and have 2.5 children. But what goals do YOU have?

1. What goals do you have for college and life?

2. Do you have written goals each year for your school year? Your job? Your relationships? Your life? How are you going to make these goals a reality?

3. What barriers to setting goals and priorities do you struggle through?

4. Do you have the habit of making a "To Do" list?
yes _____ no
> If no, why not?
> If yes, do I prioritize my list daily?

5. Do you keep time commitments consistently to:

Family & Friends	_____ yes	_____ no
Teachers	_____ yes	_____ no
Coaches	_____ yes	_____ no

6. On a scale of 1-10, 1 being best, who well do you really keep those commitments?

PRACTICAL TIPS
ON TIME IN COLLEGE

- **Go to every class!** This may sound silly, but many college freshmen sleep in or skip classes and find themselves failing finals. Often, college professors will teach material that is not in the textbook and going to lectures is the only way to know that material.

- **Shower/Hair/Shaving-** In college you may have to SHARE a bathroom with ten other girls! You may not be able to jump up at the last second and get the shower. If you spend an hour per day putting on makeup or do your hair- you need to consider that in scheduling.

- **Laundry-** if you're not taking it home on weekends for mom to do, you need about two hours per week for this task. Consider "double using" that time. Make it a social time and plan a time with friends to meet and talk or take homework that can be done with interruptions and background noise. Do low concentration items: call or write letters home or to friends or balance your checkbook or write out to do list for the week, etc.

- Sports/Music- Time to practice/train/ travel times to games. Get an accurate picture of the time spent there 4-6 hours practice daily during preseason. **Factor in the added expenses as well for extra gas, eating out, etc.**

- Weekends will be more than socializing as in high school. Your free time will be divided by responsibilities: Cleaning your dorm or apartment/ Going Grocery shopping/ Doing laundry. Be sure to save some down time to just relax and reflect on weekends when your schedule is not so demanding.

- When planning schedules for working part time while going to school consider your FULL school schedule, including homework time, not just class time

- Going away to college is a great time to clean out your closets at home! Make a keep/store seasonal/donate/trash boxes and go through your wardrobe. If you haven't worn it in six months, you probably never will. Donate it, pass it on to a friend who likes it or a kid sister, or if it is old trash it.

- Find time for quiet, reflection time in college. "Alone" time in dorm or a shared apartment is hard to find. Work out a private time when your roommate is either sleeping or in class and you have the room to yourself daily.

- Don't let your creativity die during college. How will you channel your music/art/writing/drama- that into an outlet to not let it grow stale? Your friends or youth band might not be there to jam with. You may not be in art or drama classes. Keep your creativity alive somehow! Volunteer at a local art studio or church to play music or help with art.

- DREAM TIME- You have PURPOSE in you. Find time each day/week to develop your talents and grow. If you didn't have to worry about making a living, what would you do for the rest of your life? Is your dream written down? What are the steps to accomplish it? How much time do you spend each day in accomplishing this dream?

30 minutes per day= 182 hours per year or TWENTY-TWO 8 hour working days FROM ONE YEAR of working 30 minutes per day toward that dream. In your four years at college that is 728 hours (or 4 $\frac{1}{2}$ months of 8 hour days)!

- STAY CONNECTED at home. One excellent way to maintain a good family relationship after moving from college is taking notes on your problems and situations and discuss with your parents when you go home for weekends or when you talk regularly on the phone. It is also good to have a counselor on campus or youth leader to keep open dialogue about your life and problems that arise.

XVIII.
BE A GREAT
FINISHER

QUOTE OF THE DAY
"Every instance
of time
is a pinprick
of eternity."
Marcs Aurelius

XVIII.
BE A GREAT FINISHER

"The average person goes to his grave with his music still inside him." Zig Ziglar Will YOU???

I know you are young, but we are going to do a what if?? Hopefully, this lesson will stick with you throughout life as you consider your path and help you make wiser decisions. We are gong to repeat a session from earlier in the course. Your thoughts and plans may have changed over the course of this semester.

This last assignment starts at the end of your life. If this were your last day alive, would you hold any regrets? If you continue living as you do now, when you come to the end of your earthly years, will you be satisfied that they have been spent well? Take a few minutes to answer the following probing questions. Are you on the path that will accomplish the things you hope to do with your life?

- Before I die, who do I want to be?

_____

_____

_____

_____

- Before I die, whom do I want to influence?

_____

_____

_____

- Before I die, how do I want to be used?

_____

_____

_____

_____

_____

- Before I die, what do I want people to say about me?

_____

_____

_____

_____

- What are my dreams and goals for 3-5 years from now and what am I doing today to make them a reality?

  _____

  _____

  _____

  _____

As you think about changing the world, you will do it through something unique to you. Today is a good place to begin to live in greatness.

- What am I naturally good at doing?

  _____

  _____

- What do/did I really enjoy doing as a child?

  _____

  _____

- How am I going to be who and what I want to be in life?

  _____

  _____

  _____

> *"You can get*
> *everything in life you want*
> *if you will help enough other people*
> *get what they want."*
> *Zig Ziglar*

Why I Do
the Things I Do

It may seem silly to think about the end of your life and what you will accomplish in life. It may even seem a bit corny to talk about showing love for your family and letting them know you appreciate them. You may not understand my enthusiasm for living life to the fullest and wanting to pass that flame on to another generation. There is a very good reason that "Mrs. Liz" (or Mama Liz, as many of the teens and children I've encouraged in life call me) is the way she is.

I was a very healthy, young woman of twenty-seven. Very suddenly and unexpectantly, I almost died from a colon obstruction. When I realized I had almost died, I decided to live every day as if it were my last.

What came out of that horrible experience was a new life for me. I don't know how many days I have left here on this earth, but I'm using each one as the precious gift that it is. I hope I have inspired you to use your time with greatness, too!

Don't forget—in the race of life there are 3 things to remember:

1. Keep your eyes on the finish line

2. Don't look to see what the guy next to you is doing

3. Even when you can't go on-
   FINISH the race!

As you go on in life from this course with clearly defined goals and a TO DO List in hand, learn to say NO to good things so you have TIME to do GREAT things. Be careful not to step on others as you climb the ladder of success. Remember Zig Ziglar's six things that are foundational to success: honesty, character, faith, integrity, love, and loyalty. Build them in your life.

Steward each day as if it is your last one. You never know when it might be. That way you'll never have any regrets. Finally, continue to apply 30 minutes per day to seeing that big dream in your heart become a reality!! Don't ever stop believing in yourself and don't ever give up on your dream!

BALLOONS OF GREATNESS

STEWARD Your TIME!

Live everyday as if it is your last one!

Don't EVER Give up!

Student Schooling Tips
from Time Priority Workshops©

1. **Demonstrate good time skills**- to do lists, go to class prepared, set goals, do your work with excellence.

2. **Take a few minutes on Monday** to highlight what your objective is for the week. **See what big projects are due for this week, when tests are coming, etc.**

3. **Take the initiative. Don't have to be asked to do things, take responsibility.**

4. **Are you a morning person or afternoon?** Plan complicated study tasks classes when you are mentally the strongest and most attentive.

5. **Segment your day- and stick to it!** Homework is school time- it is easier to spend ALL your time doing the schoolwork straight through than trying to run back and forth. Avoid phone calls or visitors during teaching time. It is distracting and it takes TIME to get back to the same level of concentration. Plan time in your day for friends, family, chores, and study and try to stick to a routine.

6. **Learn the concept.** Some people are conceptual learners and will learn a whole sentence rather than a word. Others are builders, memorizing one step at a time. Learn how you learn and utilize it when studying. Don't just memorize how to do it to pass a test. Subjects from year to year build on the concepts learned in previous years. If you miss the concept, you will not be able to go forward until you go back and get it, so do it right the first time.

7. **The easiest way to learn:** Watch the teacher do it, do it while the teacher watches, do it in restricted territory, then go at it alone

8. **Develop a reward system for staying on task**

9. **Find ways to express your creativity-** science projects, creative thinking skills, where one student might write a report, a creative student might draw a mural of the history of the flag, see how flexible your teacher is for a creative approach to assignments

10. **.Get a clear goal for the school year.** Check your progress monthly or quarterly. The last month of school go back and review to excel in finals or TCAPS.

11. **Variety-** music is an excellent tool to memorize make learning fun and sing what you are trying to memorize.

12. **Pattern study time around household distractions** to get a distraction free environment or go to your room and shut the door.

13. **Study with no TV or music or distractions.** Long term memory retention is lost when learning with distractions. It does not affect short-term memory so it is not so apparent.

14. **Foster healthy inter-dependence. Take on new** responsibility but not to the point you can't do it or become frustrated.

15. **Instill SUCCESS.** If you learn to love to learn, be responsible for your own progress. Set goals for yourself and suddenly you are not doing it for a teacher or parent, but yourself. you will take initiative and be more likely to be a success.

16. **Do the same thing every performance.**

17. **Get an I CAN do this attitude! Success is 90% belief.**

18 . **Don't receive rejection, but correction.**
If you don't do it right, listen to correction and don't take it personally.

19. **10% of what is taught to you is retained, 90% of what YOU teach, you retain.**
If you have younger brothers and sisters, or friends "teach" them how to do it and you will get the material more ingrained in your mind.

20. **People are different kinds of learners.** Some are audio, some are visual and need lots of illustrations and examples, while others retain better when they write it out. Find out which you are and learn the way you learn. (Spelling words- visual learner- write your words or make flash cards, audio learner, spell the words out loud)

21. **There are two kinds of learners—conceptual and factual.** You may not learn the way your brother or friends do...find your way to learn. Conceptual learners don't retain facts and figures easily...they have to understand it and the why we do it this way.

22. **Use charts! People like rewards. Make charts** for homework, chores, and eating a healthy diet.

23. Break Large Tasks into Manageable "Bites"- Take a large assignment, figure out the steps to complete it, put each step on your own daily planner with ending objective, and learn how to overcome the "mountains" in your life that is too big to move both in school and in life!

TIME 4
HIGH SCHOOL

ANSWER
KEY

TIME 4 HIGH SCHOOL
ANSWER KEY

QUIZ 1
1. *Our brain needs a pattern to follow.*
2. *B. 30%*
3. *Yourself*
4. *B*
5. *To see the most important tasks easily*
6. *21 days*
7. *A*

QUIZ 2
1. *Your plans affect their schedules and theirs affect yours*
2. *TO DO, Planning*
3. *Something you intend to do*
4. *Count the cost, believe it, say the right things, find the small steps, do it, stick with it!*
5. *5. Something you want to accomplish*

QUIZ 3
1. *30,5,3*
2. *21 days*
3. *Little, Consistency*
4. *You can "see" it before it happens*
5. *Stop and think about it*
6. *You can stay on track*

QUIZ 4
1. *A group of people about the same age*
2. *Life is more fast paced*
3. *The time when I am most productive mentally*

QUIZ 5

1. Chronos
2. 3500 B.C.
3. Tall monuments that measured sun "shadows"
4. A circle is divided into ten parts and the sun's shadow passes over it
5. Using a Merkhet and the stars, Water clock

QUIZ 6

1. 364 ¼ days
2. The moon cycle did not divide evenly
3. Eqyptians
4. A calendar of 30 or 31 day months with a day added in February for leap year

QUIZ 7

1. 86,400
2. 2-3 hours, 3 hours
3. Results you want to see
4. Sand passes from one bubble of glass to another through a narrow tube at a predictable rate
5. A chart to record where my time is spent

QUIZ 8

1. 100 hours
2. When you know how much time you have it keeps you more focused
3. Something of value
4. Precious
5. Save, spend
6. Lack, use

QUIZ 9

1. Doing something without being told
2. John Quincy Adams
3. The small stake held them when they were little elephants, and they don't know it can't hold them anymore
4. Greatness is on the inside of you

QUIZ 10

1. 4
2. 5
3. Together Everyone Accomplishes Much
4. Thief
5. To put off doing something
5. Salami technique, 15 minute approach, Ben Franklin approach

QUIZ 11

1. The brain was designed to function in structure
2. 1/3
3. Long term
4. The brain needs a pattern to follow
5. It makes you feel good
6. Don't spread yourself too thin, plan ahead

QUIZ 12

1. Internal and External
2. 18,000 hours
3. Reflect
4. Parents, Teachers, Youth Leader, School Counselor
5. TV, Video games, Social distractions
6. Procrastination, Stress
7. Reset inner clock, good sleep, write it down, talk to parents, reduce load

Daily Plans for_____

Time is SHORT! Live today like it could be your last!

Today's Agenda:

8 AM_____	12PM_____	4 PM_____	8 PM_____
9 AM_____	1 PM_____	5 PM_____	9 PM_____
10AM_____	2 PM_____	6 PM_____	10PM_____
11AM_____	3 PM_____	7 PM_____	11PM_____

Music/Sports Practice Times Today_____

Concerts/Games Today_____

Assignments Due Today

_____

_____

_____

_____

_____

_____

_____

_____

Tests Today

_____

_____

_____

_____

_____

_____

New Assignments- from Today's Classes   *Due Date*

_____
_____
_____
_____
_____
_____
_____
_____
_____

Homework To Work on Today   *Due Date*

_____
_____
_____
_____
_____
_____

Social/Community Agenda Today

_____
_____
_____

Personal Stuff to do

_____
_____
_____

Other Books by Elizabeth Franklin

THE WARRIOR KIDS SERIES-Fiction adventure series- Come join the Warrior Kids as they uncover keys to open Kingdom Treasures www.warriorkidsclub.com

TIME 4 KIDS and TEENS© 2009
A Time management course for older elementary to middle school age students in both traditional and Christian edition.

TIME 4 COLLEGE© 2007
A Pre-College or College Student Workshop on TIME. www.timepriorityworkshops.com

"I Miss My Time with You"-Time Priority paperback that emerged from author Elizabeth Franklin's own personal brush with death in 1984 and the lifestyle changes that came from that experience. www.timepriorityworkshops.com

Also, check out my daughter's new series! Presenting ten-year-old author and illustrator, Anna Franklin's and Pentelope the Penguin!
Pentelope Penguin at **www.pentelopepenguin.org**

TIME 4 MOMS, COLLEGE, KIDS, and TEENS WORKSHOPS www.itstime4u.org
Find other time and motivational materials at www.TIME2BGREAT.com

37570933R00150

Made in the USA
Middletown, DE
28 February 2019